# AWS Secrets Manager User Guide

A catalogue record for this book is available from the Hong Kong Public Libraries.

Published in Hong Kong by Samurai Media Limited.

Email: info@samuraimedia.org

ISBN 9789888408818

# Contents

## Troubleshooting AWS Secrets Manager ..... **151**

# What Is AWS Secrets Manager?

AWS Secrets Manager is an AWS service that makes it easier for you to manage secrets. *Secrets* can be database credentials, passwords, third-party API keys, and even arbitrary text. You can store and control access to these secrets centrally by using the Secrets Manager console, the Secrets Manager command line interface (CLI), or the Secrets Manager API and SDKs.

In the past, when you created a custom application that retrieves information from a database, you typically had to embed the credentials (the secret) for accessing the database directly in the application. When it came time to rotate the credentials, you had to do much more than just create new credentials. You had to invest time to update the application to use the new credentials. Then you had to distribute the updated application. If you had multiple applications that shared credentials and you missed updating one of them, the application would break. Because of this risk, many customers have chosen not to regularly rotate their credentials, which effectively substitutes one risk for another.

Secrets Manager enables you to replace hardcoded credentials in your code (including passwords), with an API call to Secrets Manager to retrieve the secret programmatically. This helps ensure that the secret can't be compromised by someone examining your code, because the secret simply isn't there. Also, you can configure Secrets Manager to automatically rotate the secret for you according to a schedule that you specify. This enables you to replace long-term secrets with short-term ones, which helps to significantly reduce the risk of compromise.

## Getting Started with Secrets Manager

For a list of terms and concepts that you need to understand to make full use of Secrets Manager, see Key Terms and Concepts for AWS Secrets Manager.

Typical users of Secrets Manager fall into one or more of the following roles:

- Secrets Manager administrator – Administers the Secrets Manager service. Grants permissions to individuals who can then perform the other roles listed here.
- Database or service administrator – Administers the database or service whose secrets are stored in Secrets Manager. Determines and configures the rotation and expiration settings for the secrets they own.
- Application developer – Creates the application, and configures it to request the appropriate credentials from Secrets Manager.

## Basic Secrets Manager Scenario

The following diagram illustrates the most basic scenario. It shows how you can store credentials for a database in Secrets Manager, and then use those credentials in an application that needs to access the database.

1. The database administrator creates a set of credentials on the Personnel database for use by an app called MyCustomApp. The administrator also configures those credentials with the permissions that are required for the app to access the Personnel database.

2. The database administrator stores those credentials as a secret in Secrets Manager named *MyCustomApp-Creds*. The credentials are encrypted and stored within the secret as the *protected secret text*.

3. When MyCustomApp needs to access the database, the app queries Secrets Manager for the secret named *MyCustomAppCreds*.

4. Secrets Manager retrieves the secret, decrypts the protected secret text, and returns it to the client app over a secured (HTTPS with TLS) channel.

5. The client app parses the credentials, connection string, and any other required information from the response and then uses that information to access the database server.

**Note**

Secrets Manager knows how to work with many types of secrets. However, Secrets Manager can *natively* rotate credentials for select AWS databases without requiring any additional programming. However, rotating the secrets for other databases or services requires you to create a custom Lambda function to define how Secrets Manager interacts with the database or service. You need some programming skill to create that function. For more information, see Rotating Your AWS Secrets Manager Secrets.

## Features of Secrets Manager

### Programmatically Retrieve Encrypted Secret Values at Runtime Instead of Storing Them

One of the most important reasons to use Secrets Manager is to help you improve your security posture by removing hard-coded credentials from your app's source code, and by not storing credentials in or with the app itself, in any way. Storing the credentials in or with the app subjects them to possible compromise by anyone who can inspect your app or its components. It also makes rotating your credentials difficult at best. This is because you have to update your app and deploy the changes to every client before you can deprecate the old credentials.

Secrets Manager enables you to replace stored credentials with a runtime call to the Secrets Manager web service, so you can retrieve the credentials dynamically when you need them.

Most of the time, your client simply wants to access the most recent version of the encrypted secret value. When you query for the encrypted secret value, you can choose to provide only the secret's name or Amazon Resource Name (ARN), without specifying any version information at all. If you do this, Secrets Manager automatically returns the most recent version of the secret value.

However, other versions can exist at the same time. Most systems support secrets that are more complicated than a simple password—such as full sets of credentials that include the connection details, the user ID, and the password. Secrets Manager allows you to have multiple sets of these credentials that exist at the same time. Each set is stored in a different version of the secret. During the secret rotation process, Secrets Manager tracks the older credentials that you're replacing, as well as the new credentials that you want to start using, until the rotation is complete. It tracks these different versions by using *staging labels*.

### Store Just About Any Kind of Secret

Secrets Manager enables you to store text up to 4096 bytes in length in the encrypted secret data portion of a secret. This typically includes the connection details of the database or service. These details can include the server name, IP address, and port number, as well as the user name and password that are used to sign in to the service. The protected text doesn't include the secret name and description, the rotation or expiration settings, the ARN of the AWS KMS customer master key that's used to encrypt and decrypt the secret, or any AWS tags that you might attach.

Secrets Manager encrypts the protected text of a secret by using AWS Key Management Service (AWS KMS), a key storage and encryption service that's used by many AWS services. This helps ensure that your secret is securely encrypted when it's at rest. In addition, Secrets Manager, by default, only accepts requests from hosts that use the open standard Transport Layer Security (TLS) and Perfect Forward Secrecy. This helps ensure that your secret is also encrypted while it's in transit between AWS and the computers that you use to retrieve the secret.

Secrets Manager can use a default AWS KMS customer master key (CMK) that you own and control for all of the secrets in your account. Or you can specify individual CMKs for any secrets that require a different key.

### Automatically Rotate Your Secrets

You can configure Secrets Manager to automatically rotate your secrets without any user intervention and on a schedule that you specify.

You define and implement rotation with an AWS Lambda function. This function defines how Secrets Manager creates a new version of the secret, stores it in Secrets Manager, configures the protected service to use the new version, verifies that the new version works, and then marks the new version as production ready.

Staging labels help you to keep track of the different versions of your secrets. Each version can have multiple staging labels attached, but a given staging label can be attached to only one version. For example, the currently active and in-use version of the secret is labeled AWSCURRENT. Your apps typically should be configured to always query for that version of the secret. When the rotation process creates a new version of a secret, it automatically adds the staging label AWSPENDING to the new version until it's tested and validated. Only then does Secrets Manager move the AWSCURRENT staging label to this new version. Your apps immediately start using the new secret the next time they query for the AWSCURRENT version.

### Databases with Fully Configured and Ready-to-Use Rotation Support

When you choose to enable rotation, the following Amazon Relational Database Service (Amazon RDS) databases are fully supported with AWS written and tested Lambda rotation function templates, and full configuration of the rotation process:

- Amazon Aurora
- MySQL
- PostgreSQL

You can also store secrets for almost any other kind of database or service. However, to automatically rotate them you'll need to create and configure a custom Lambda rotation function yourself. For more information about writing a custom Lambda function for a database or service, see Overview of the Lambda Rotation Function.

### Control Who Can Access Secrets

You can attach AWS Identity and Access Management (IAM) permission policies to your users, groups, and roles that grant or deny access to specific secrets, and restrict what they can do with those secrets. For example, you might attach one policy to a group whose members need the ability to fully manage and configure your secrets. Another policy attached to a role that's used by an application might grant only read permission on the one secret that the application needs to run.

## Compliance with Standards

AWS Secrets Manager has undergone auditing for the following standards and can be part of your solution when you need to obtain compliance certification.

AWS has expanded its Health Insurance Portability and Accountability Act (HIPAA) compliance program to include AWS Secrets Manager as a HIPAA Eligible Service. If you have an executed Business Associate Agreement (BAA) with AWS, you can use Secrets Manager to help build your HIPAA-compliant applications. AWS offers a HIPAA-focused Whitepaper for customers who are interested in learning more about how they can leverage AWS for the processing and storage of health information. For more information, see HIPAA Compliance

## Accessing Secrets Manager

You can work with Secrets Manager in any of the following ways:

### AWS Management Console
The Secrets Manager console is a browser-based interface that you can use to manage your secrets. You can perform almost any task that's related to your secrets by using the console.

Currently, you can't do the following in the console:

- *Store binary data in a secret.* The console currently stores data only in the `SecureString` field of the secret, and doesn't use the `SecureBinary` field. To store binary data, you must currently use the AWS CLI or one of the AWS SDKs.

### AWS Command Line Tools
The AWS command line tools let you issue commands at your system's command line to perform Secrets Manager and other AWS tasks. This can be faster and more convenient than using the console. The command line tools also are useful if you want to build scripts that perform AWS tasks.

AWS provides two sets of command line tools: the AWS Command Line Interface (AWS CLI) and the AWS Tools for Windows PowerShell. For information about installing and using the AWS CLI, see the AWS Command Line Interface User Guide. For information about installing and using the Tools for Windows PowerShell, see the AWS Tools for Windows PowerShell User Guide.

### AWS SDKs
The AWS SDKs consist of libraries and sample code for various programming languages and platforms (for example, Java, Python, Ruby, .NET, iOS and Android, and others). The SDKs include tasks such as cryptographically signing requests, managing errors, and retrying requests automatically. For more information about the AWS SDKs, including how to download and install them, see Tools for Amazon Web Services.

### Secrets Manager HTTPS Query API

The Secrets Manager HTTPS Query API gives you programmatic access to Secrets Manager and AWS. The HTTPS Query API lets you issue HTTPS requests directly to the service. When you use the HTTPS API, you must include code to digitally sign requests by using your credentials. For more information, see Calling the API by Making HTTP Query Requests and the AWS Secrets Manager API Reference.

We recommend that you use the SDK that's specific to the programming language you prefer instead of using the HTTPS Query API. The SDK performs many useful tasks that you otherwise must do manually. One example is that the SDKs automatically sign your requests and convert the response into a structure that's syntactically appropriate to your language. Use the HTTPS Query API only when an SDK isn't available.

## Pricing for Secrets Manager

When you use Secrets Manager, you pay only for what you use, and there are no minimum or setup fees. For the current complete pricing list, see AWS Secrets Manager Pricing.

### AWS KMS – Custom Encryption Keys

If you create your own customer master keys by using AWS KMS to encrypt your secrets, then you're charged at the current AWS KMS rate. However, you can use the "default" key that AWS Secrets Manager creates for your account for free. For more information about the cost of customer-created AWS KMS keys, see AWS Key Management Service Pricing.

### AWS CloudTrail Logging – Storage and Notification

If you enable AWS CloudTrail on your account, you can obtain logs of API calls that AWS Secrets Manager makes. There's no additional charge for AWS CloudTrail. However, you can incur charges for Amazon S3 for log storage and for Amazon SNS if you enable notification. For more information, see the AWS CloudTrail pricing page.

# Support and Feedback for AWS Secrets Manager

We welcome your feedback. You can send comments to awssecretsmanager-feedback@amazon.com. You also can post your feedback and questions in our AWS Secrets Manager support forum. For more information about the AWS Support forums, see Forums Help.

To make feature requests for the AWS Secrets Manager console or command line tools, we recommend that you submit them in email to awssecretsmanager-feedback@amazon.com.

To provide feedback for our documentation, you can use the feedback link at the bottom of each webpage. Be specific about the issue you're facing and how the documentation failed to help you. Let us know what you saw and how that differed from what you expected. That'll help us to understand what we need to do to improve the documentation.

Here are some additional resources that are available to you:

- **AWS Training Catalog** – Role-based and specialty courses, as well as self-paced labs, to help you sharpen your AWS skills and gain practical experience.
- **AWS Developer Tools** – Tools and resources that provide documentation, code examples, release notes, and other information to help you build innovative applications with AWS.
- **AWS Support Center** – The hub for creating and managing your AWS Support cases. It includes links to other helpful resources, such as forums, technical FAQs, service health status, and AWS Trusted Advisor.
- **AWS Support** – A one-on-one, fast-response support channel for helping you build and run applications in the cloud.
- **Contact Us** – A central contact point for inquiries about AWS billing, accounts, events, and other issues.
- **AWS Site Terms** – Detailed information about our copyright and trademark, your account, your license, site access, and other topics.

# Getting Started with AWS Secrets Manager

To get started using AWS Secrets Manager, we recommend that you review the following topics:

- Terms and Concepts - Basic concepts and Secrets Manager terms that we use throughout the APIs, SDK commands, and the console interface.
- Tutorials - Step-by-step procedures that walk you through common scenarios to teach you how to do basic tasks in Secrets Manager.

# Key Terms and Concepts for AWS Secrets Manager

The following terms and concepts are important for understanding AWS Secrets Manager and how it works.

## Secret

In Secrets Manager, a secret is typically a set of credentials (user name and password) and the connection details that you use to access a secured service. You want to store these securely, and ensure that only authorized users can access them. Secrets Manager always stores the secret text in an encrypted form and encrypts the secret in transit.

Secrets Manager uses IAM permission policies to ensure that only authorized users can access or modify the secret. You can attach these policies to users or roles, and specify which secrets those users can access. For more details about controlling access to your secrets, see Authentication and Access Control for AWS Secrets Manager.

When storing credentials, different secured services might require different pieces of information. Secrets Manager provides this flexibility by storing the secret as key-value pairs of text strings. If you choose a database that Secrets Manager knows how to work with, then the key-value pairs are defined for you according to the requirements of the rotation function for the chosen database. The pairs are formatted as JSON text. If you choose some other service or database that Secrets Manager doesn't provide the Lambda function for, then you can specify your secret as JSON key-value pairs that you define.

The resulting stored encrypted secret text might then resemble the following example:

```
1 {
2   "host" : "ProdServer-01.databases.example.com",
3   "port" : "8888",
4   "username"    : "administrator",
5   "password"    : "My-P@ssw0rd!F0r+Th3_Acc0unt",
6   "dbname"      : "MyDatabase",
7   "engine"      : "mysql"
8 }
```

If you use the command-line tools or the API, you can also store binary data in the secret. Binary data isn't supported by the Secrets Manager console.

Secrets Manager can automatically rotate your secret for you on a schedule that you specify. You can rotate credentials without interrupting the service if you choose to store a complete set of credentials for a user or account, instead of only the password. If you change or rotate only the password, then the old password immediately becomes obsolete, and clients must immediately start using the new password or fail. If you can instead create a new user with a new password, or at least alternate between two users, then the old user and password can continue to operate side by side with the new one, until you choose to deprecate the old one. This gives you a window of time where all of your clients can continue to work while you test and validate the new credentials. Only after your new credentials pass testing do you commit all of your clients to using the new credentials and remove the old credentials.

### Supported Databases
If you use the Secrets Manager console and specify that the secret is for one of the databases that Secrets Manager natively supports, then Secrets Manager manages all of that structure and parsing for you. The console prompts you for the details that the specific type of database needs. Behind the scenes, Secrets Manager constructs the structure that's needed, stores the information, and then parses it back into easy-to-understand text information when you retrieve it.

### Other Databases or Services
If you instead specify that the secret is for a "custom" database or service, then what you do with the secret text after you retrieve it and how you interpret it is up to you. The Secrets Manager console accepts your secret as key-value strings, and automatically converts them into a JSON structure for storage. If you retrieve the secret

in the console, Secrets Manager automatically parses the secret back into key-value text strings for you to view. If you retrieve the secret programmatically, then you can use an appropriate JSON parsing library (available for almost every programming language), to parse the secret in any way that's useful to you. If a secret requires more than per-secret limit of 4096 characters to store, you could split your key-value pairs between two secrets and concatenate them back together when you retrieve them.

**Basic Structure of a Secrets Manager Secret**

In Secrets Manager, a secret contains not only the encrypted secret text, but also several metadata elements that describe the secret and define how Secrets Manager should handle the secret:

## Secret

| ARN | Rotation configuration |
| Name | Last used date/time stamps |
| Description | Tags[] |
| KMSKeyId | |

| **Version** | **Version** | **Version** |
|---|---|---|
| ID | ID | ID |
| Staging labels[] | Staging labels[] | Staging labels[] |
| Secret value | Secret value | Secret value |

- **Metadata – Details about the secret**
  - Basic information that includes the name of the secret, a description, and the Amazon Resource Name (ARN) that serves as a unique identifier.
  - The ARN of the AWS Key Management Service (AWS KMS) key that Secrets Manager uses to encrypt and decrypt the protected text in the secret. If this isn't present, Secrets Manager uses the default AWS KMS key for the account.
  - Information about how frequently the key is automatically rotated and what Lambda function to use to perform the rotation.
  - A user-provided set of tags. Tags are key-value pairs that you can attach to AWS resources for organizing, logical grouping, and cost allocation.
- **Versions – A collection of one or more versions of the encrypted secret text**
  - Although you typically only have one version of the secret active at a time, multiple versions can exist while you rotate a secret on the database or service. A new version is created whenever you need to change the secret, such as when you change the password.
  - Each version holds its own copy of the encrypted secret value.
  - Each version can have one or more staging labels attached that identify where that version is in the secret's rotation cycle.

## Secured Service

The secured service is the service, such as a database or other service running on a network server, whose access is controlled by the credentials stored in the secret. The secured service can refer to a single server or a large group of servers that all share the same access method. You need the secret to successfully access the secured service. The secret contains all of the information that a client needs to access the secured service. This guide uses the term "secured service" as a generic term to represent all of the different types of databases and services whose secrets can be protected by AWS Secrets Manager.

## Rotation

Rotation is the process where you periodically change the secret to make it more difficult for an attacker to access the secured service. With Secrets Manager, you don't have to manually change the secret and update it on all of your clients. Instead, Secrets Manager uses an AWS Lambda function to perform all of the steps of rotation for you on a regular schedule.

Imagine a large set of clients that are all running an application that accesses a database (the secured service). Instead of hardcoding the credentials into your app, the app calls Secrets Manager to request the secret's details whenever they're needed. When it's time to rotate the secret, the Lambda rotation function automatically performs the following steps:

1. The rotation function contacts the secured service's authentication system and creates a new set of credentials to access the database. The credentials typically consist of a user name, a password, and connection details, but can vary from system to system. Secrets Manager stores these new credentials as the secret text in a new version of the secret that gets the AWSPENDING staging label attached.

2. The rotation function then tests the AWSPENDING version of the secret to ensure that the credentials work, and that they grant the required level of access to the secured service.

3. If the tests succeed, the rotation function then moves the label AWSCURRENT to the new version to mark it as the "default" version. This causes all of the clients to start using this version of the secret instead of the old version. The function also assigns the label AWSPREVIOUS to the old version, which marks it as the "last known good" version. The version that previously had the AWSPREVIOUS staging label now has none, and is therefore deprecated.

You can trigger the Lambda rotation function manually when you choose **Rotate secret** in the console, or you can trigger it automatically every *n* days by specifying a rotation schedule. If you use one of the AWS databases that Secrets Manager natively supports, then Secrets Manager provides a Lambda function that knows how to rotate that database's credentials. This function performs basic rotation for you automatically or you can customize the function to support an advanced custom rotation strategy.

If you choose to create a secret for a custom service, then you must create the Lambda function yourself. In the code of the function, you determine how to compose the JSON structure and parse it in your function.

For more information about rotation, see Rotating Your AWS Secrets Manager Secrets.

## Version

Multiple versions of a secret exist to support rotation of a secret. Different versions are distinguished by their staging labels. For most scenarios, you don't have to worry about versions of the secret. Secrets Manager and the provided Lambda rotation function manage these details for you. However, if you create your own Lambda rotation function, your code must manage multiple versions of a secret and move the staging labels between versions appropriately. Versions also each have a unique identifier (typically a UUID value) that always stays with the same version, unlike staging labels that you can move between versions.

You typically configure your clients to always ask for the "default" version of the secret. This is the version that has the AWSCURRENT label attached. Other versions can exist, but they're only accessed if you specifically request a specific version ID or staging label. If you ask for the secret value and you don't specify either a version ID or a staging label, then by default you get the version with the staging label AWSCURRENT.

During rotation, Secrets Manager creates a new version of the secret and attaches the staging label AWSPENDING. The rotation function uses the AWSPENDING version to identify that version until it passes testing. After the rotation function verifies that the new credentials work, it moves the label `AWSPREVIOUS` to the older version that has `AWSCURRENT`, moves the label `AWSCURRENT` to the newer `AWSPENDING` version, and finally removes `AWSPENDING`.

For more information about how staging labels work to support rotation, see Rotating Your AWS Secrets Manager Secrets.

Each version that's maintained for a secret has the following elements:

- A unique ID for the version.
- A collection of staging labels that can be used to identify the version (unique within the secret). A version with no staging labels is considered deprecated and subject to deletion by Secrets Manager.
- The secret text that's encrypted and stored.

Whenever you query for the encrypted secret value, you can specify the version of the secret that you want. If you don't specify a version (either by version ID or staging label), Secrets Manager defaults to the version with the staging label `AWSCURRENT` attached. This is the one staging label that's guaranteed to always be attached to one version of the secret.

## Staging Label

Secrets Manager uses staging labels to enable you to identify different versions of a secret during rotation. A staging label is a simple text string. Whenever you query for the encrypted secret value, you can specify the version of the secret that you want. If you don't specify a version (either by version ID or staging label), Secrets Manager defaults to the version with the staging label `AWSCURRENT` attached. This is the one staging label that's guaranteed to always be attached to one version of the secret. See the brief introduction to rotation for an example of how this can work.

A version of a secret can have from 0 to 20 staging labels attached.

A staging label can be attached to only one version of a secret at a time. Two versions of the secret can't have the same staging label. When you attach a staging label to a version and it's already attached to a different version, you must also specify the version it needs to be removed from, or you get an error.

One version of the secret must **always** have the staging label `AWSCURRENT`. This is enforced by the API operations. The Lambda rotation functions that are provided by Secrets Manager automatically maintain the `AWSPENDING`, `AWSCURRENT`, and `AWSPREVIOUS` labels on the appropriate versions.

# AWS Secrets Manager Tutorials

Use the tutorials in this section to learn how to perform tasks using AWS Secrets Manager.

Tutorial: Storing and Retrieving a Secret
Get up and running with step-by-step instructions to create a secret and then retrieve it.

Tutorial: Rotating a Secret for an AWS Database
Create a secret for an Amazon RDS MySQL database. Then rotate the secret that's used to access the database, and configure it to rotate on a schedule.

Tutorial: Rotating a User Secret with a Master Secret
Use the previous tutorial's secret as a *master* secret that can rotate a separate *user* secret for an Amazon RDS MySQL database. Then rotate the user secret by signing in as the master secret and alternating users.

# Tutorial: Storing and Retrieving a Secret

In this tutorial, you create a secret and store it in AWS Secrets Manager. You then retrieve it in both the AWS Management Console and the AWS CLI.

**Step 1: Create and Store Your Secret in AWS Secrets Manager**
In this step, you create a secret and provide the basic information that AWS Secrets Manager requires.

**Step 2: Retrieve Your Secret from AWS Secrets Manager**
Next, you use the Secrets Manager console and the AWS CLI to retrieve the decoded secret.

## Prerequisites

This tutorial assumes that you have access to an AWS account. It also assumes that you can sign in to AWS as an IAM user with permissions to create and retrieve secrets in the AWS Secrets Manager console, or use equivalent commands in the AWS CLI.

## Step 1: Create and Store Your Secret in AWS Secrets Manager

In this step, you sign in as an IAM user and create a secret.

**To create and store your secret**

1. Sign in to the AWS Secrets Manager console at https://console.aws.amazon.com/secretsmanager/.

2. On either the service introduction page or the secrets list page, choose **Store a new secret**.

3. On the **Store a new secret** page, choose **Other type of secret**.

4. For **Select the encryption key**, choose **DefaultEncryptionKey**. You aren't charged by AWS KMS if you use the default AWS managed key that Secrets Manager creates in your account. If you choose to use a KMS key that you created, then you can be charged at the standard AWS KMS rate.

5. Under **Credentials you want to store**, choose **Secret key : Secret value** so that you can type the secret as key-value pairs.

6. In the first text box, type **username**. In the second box, type: **myserviceusername**.

7. Choose **+Add row** to add a second key-value pair.

8. In the first box, type **password**. In the second box, type: **MyVerySecureP@ssw0rd!**.

9. Choose **Plaintext** above the boxes to see the JSON version of the secret text that will be stored in the `SecretString` field of the secret.

10. For **Select the encryption key**, leave it set at the default value **DefaultEncryptionKey**.

11. Choose **Next**.

12. Under **Secret name and description**, for **Secret name**, type **tutorials/MyFirstTutorialSecret**. This stores your secret in the virtual folder "tutorials".

13. For **Description**, type something like: **The secret I created for the first tutorial.**

14. Choose **Next**.

15. In this tutorial, we don't use rotation, so choose **Disable automatic rotation**, and then choose **Next**.

16. On the **Review** page, you can check all of the settings you chose. Also, be sure to review the **Sample code** section that has cut-and-paste–enabled code that you can put into your own apps to use this secret to retrieve the credentials. Each tab has the same code in different programming languages.

17. To save your changes, choose **Store**.

You're returned to the list of secrets in your account with your new secret now included in the list.

## Step 2: Retrieve Your Secret from AWS Secrets Manager

In this step, you retrieve the secret by using both the Secrets Manager console and the AWS CLI.

**To retrieve your secret in the AWS Secrets Manager console**

1. On the secrets list page, choose the name of the new secret that you created in the previous section.

   The details page for your secret appears.

2. In the **Credential data** section, choose **Retrieve secret value**.

3. You can view your secret as either key-value pairs, or as a JSON text structure.

**To retrieve your secret by using the AWS Secrets Manager CLI**

1. Open a command prompt where you can run the AWS CLI. If you haven't installed the AWS CLI yet, see Installing the AWS Command Line Interface.

2. Using credentials that have permissions to access your secret, type each of the following commands.

   **To see all of the details of your secret except the encrypted text:**

```
1  $ aws secretsmanager describe-secret --secret-id tutorials/MyFirstTutorialSecret
2  {
3      "ARN": "arn:aws:secretsmanager:region:123456789012:secret:tutorials/
           MyFirstTutorialSecret-jiObOV",
4      "Name": "tutorials/MyFirstTutorialSecret",
5      "Description": "My First Secret",
6      "LastChangedDate": 1522680794.8,
7      "LastAccessedDate": 1522627200.0,
8      "VersionIdsToStages": {
9          "EXAMPLE1-90ab-cdef-fedc-ba987EXAMPLE": [
10             "AWSCURRENT"
11         ]
12     }
13 }
```

   One item to pay attention to is the **VersionIdsToStages** response value. This contains a list of all of the active versions of the secret and the staging labels that are attached to each version. In this tutorial, you should see one version ID (a UUID type value) that maps to a single staging label AWSCURRENT.

   **To see the encrypted text in your secret:**

```
1  $ aws secretsmanager get-secret-value --secret-id tutorials/MyFirstTutorialSecret --version
      -stage AWSCURRENT
2  {
3      "ARN": "arn:aws:secretsmanager:region:123456789012:secret:tutorials/
           MyFirstTutorialSecret-jiObOV",
4      "Name": "tutorials/MyFirstTutorialSecret",
5      "VersionId": "EXAMPLE1-90ab-cdef-fedc-ba987EXAMPLE",
6      "SecretString": "{\"username\":\"myserviceusername\",\"password\":\"
           MyVerySecureP@ssw0rd!\"}",
7      "VersionStages": [
8          "AWSCURRENT"
9      ],
```

```
10        "CreatedDate": 1522680764.668
11  }
```

Actually, you need to include the `--version-stage` parameter in the previous command only if you want details for a version with a different staging label than `AWSCURRENT`. `AWSCURRENT` is the default value.

The result includes the JSON version of your secret value in the `SecretString` response field.

**Summary**

This tutorial demonstrated how easy it is to create a simple secret, and to retrieve the secret value whenever it's needed. For another tutorial that shows how to create a secret and configure it to automatically rotate, see Tutorial: Rotating a Secret for an AWS Database.

# Tutorial: Rotating a Secret for an AWS Database

In this tutorial, you create a secret for an AWS database and configure it to rotate on a schedule. You trigger one rotation manually, and then confirm that the new version of the secret continues to provide access.

### Step 1: Set Up a Test Database
In this step, you create a test database in Amazon Relational Database Service (Amazon RDS). For this tutorial, the test database runs MySQL.

### Step 2: Create Your Secret
Next, you use the Secrets Manager console to create your secret and populate it with the initial user name and password for your MySQL database. You test the secret by using the returned credentials to sign in to the database.

### Step 3: Validate Your Initial Secret
In step 3, you use your new secret to test the credentials and ensure that you can use them to connect to your database.

### Step 4: Configure Rotation for Your Secret
In step 4, you enable rotation for the secret and perform the initial rotation.

### Step 5: Verify Successful Rotation
In this step, after the initial rotation completes, you repeat the validation steps to show that the new credentials generated during rotation continue to allow you to access the database.

### Step 6: Clean Up
In the final step, we remove the Amazon RDS database instance and the secret to avoid incurring any unnecessary costs.

## Prerequisites

This tutorial assumes that you have access to an AWS account. It also assumes that you can sign in to AWS as a user with full permissions to operate AWS Secrets Manager and Amazon RDS, in either the console or by using the equivalent commands in the AWS CLI.

The tutorial uses a MySQL client tool to interact with the database and configure users, and to check status. The installation instructions are shown at the appropriate point in the steps that follow.

The tutorial also uses a Linux JSON parsing tool called **jq**. To download the tool, see jq on the GitHub website.

**Important**
For the sake of simplicity, this tutorial uses jq to parse the secret value into environment variables to allow for easy command line manipulation. This is NOT a security best practice for a production environment. In a production environment, we recommend that you don't store passwords in environment variables, and work with them in plaintext at the command line.
Also, the database that's configured in this tutorial is open to the public internet on port 3306, again for simplicity in setup for the tutorial. The Lambda function must be able to access both the public AWS Secrets Manager service endpoint and your database. Making the database publicly accessible is the easiest way to do this. However, it's not the most secure way. Follow the guidance in the Lambda and Amazon EC2 VPC documentation to securely configure your production services and database.

## Step 1: Set Up a Test Database

In this step, you sign in to your account and set up a MySQL database in Amazon RDS.

1. Sign in to the AWS Management Console and open the Amazon RDS console at https://console.aws.amazon.com/rds/.

2. If you see the **Amazon Relational Database Service** welcome page, choose **Get started now**.

   If you see your dashboard, choose **Instances**, and then choose **Launch DB instance**.

3. On the **Select engine** page, choose **MySQL**, select **Only enable options eligible for RDS Free Usage Tier**, and then choose **Next**.

4. On the **Specify DB details** page, in the **Instance specifications** section, leave all of the settings at their default values.

5. In the **Settings** section, make the following choices:

   - **DB instance identifier**: MyTestDatabaseInstance
   - **Master username**: adminuser.
   - **Master password**: Type a secure initial password, and repeat it in the **Confirm password** box. *Be sure to remember this password.* You'll need it when you create your secret in Step 2.

6. Choose **Next**.

7. On the **Configure advanced settings** page, in the **Network & Security** section, set **Public accessibility** to **Yes**. This setting automatically adds a public Elastic IP address to the database instance. There's no requirement to attach the VPC to the Lambda rotation function. Leave all other network settings on their default values. **Note**
   These settings are the minimal settings you need to get the tutorial working. If you require the use of a private VPC, then you must attach a NAT gateway to the VPC to allow the VPC to access the Secrets Manager service endpoint on the public internet. The routing tables from your subnets must route internet requests to the NAT gateway. The security group rules must allow incoming traffic to your database on the configured port number. You must also attach the Lambda rotation function created in Step 4 to the VPC so that the function can communicate with the database. For more information about how to configure a VPC with subnets and security groups, see the Amazon VPC User Guide.

8. In the **Database options** section, for **Database name**, type **MyTestDatabase**. Leave the other settings at default values.

9. In the **Backup** section, set the **Backup retention** period to **0 days** to disable backups.

10. Leave the settings in all other sections at their default values.

11. Choose **Launch DB instance**. Wait until the instance is up and running before proceeding with the next step. It can take several minutes to complete.

12. When the **Summary** section's **DB instance status** shows as **Available**, refresh the page, and then scroll down to the **Connect** section.

13. In the **Connect** section, choose the name of the security group that is of the type **CIDR/IP - Inbound**. This opens the Amazon EC2 console for that security group.

14. At the bottom of the page, choose the **Inbound** tab, and then choose **Edit**.

    There's one existing rule that enables access to the database from the current VPC. You need enable access to the database from the public internet, so that both the Lambda function and your eventual customers running apps can all access this database. **Warning**
    The following step opens up your test database to the internet. This isn't a secure configuration, but is provided here to make the configuration steps for this tutorial simpler. For a secure setup, you should not make your VPC accessible to the public internet. Instead, configure your VPC with a NAT gateway. When you then configure your secret to rotate, the Lambda function that Secrets Manager creates is configured to run in your VPC. You need a NAT gateway to enable the Lambda function to access the Secrets Manager service on the internet. When you're done with these tutorials on this database, we recommend that you remove the rule that you create in the next step.

15. Under **Source**, change it from **Custom** to **Anywhere**. Leave the Port Range at **3306**, which is the default for MySQL.

16. Choose **Save**.

## Step 2: Create Your Secret

In this step, you create a secret in Secrets Manager, and populate it with the details of your test database and the credentials of your master user.

1. Open the Secrets Manager console at https://console.aws.amazon.com/secretsmanager/.

2. Ensure that your console is set to the same region as you created the Amazon RDS MySQL database in the previous step.

3. Choose **Store a new secret**.

4. On the **Create Secret** page, in the **Select secret type** section, choose **Credentials for RDS database**.

5. For **User name**, type **adminuser** to match the name of the master user that you previously provided in Step 1.5.

6. For **Password**, type the same password that you provided for **adminuser** in Step 1.5.

7. For **Select the encryption key**, leave it set to **DefaultEncryptionKey**.

8. For **Select which RDS database this secret will access**, choose the instance **MyTestDatabaseInstance** that you created in Step 1.

9. Choose **Next**.

10. In the **Secret name and description** section, for **Secret name**, type **MyTestDatabaseMasterSecret**.

11. In the **Configure automatic rotation** section, leave rotation disabled for now. Choose **Next**.

12. In the **Review** section, verify your details, and then choose **Store**.

    You're returned to the list of secrets, which now includes your new secret.

## Step 3: Validate Your Initial Secret

Before you configure your secret to rotate automatically, you should verify that the information in your secret is correct and can be used to connect to the database. In this tutorial, we describe how to install a Linux-based MySQL client component. Then we run a Linux command that retrieves the secret and connects to the database using the credentials it finds in the secret.

If you're running this tutorial on some other platform, you might have to translate these commands into equivalents for your platform. At the very least, you can retrieve the secret by using either the AWS CLI or the Secrets Manager console. Then cut and paste the user name and password into whatever MySQL database client you use.

1. Install a MySQL client. For example:

```
1 $ sudo yum install mysql
2 ...
3 Installed:
4   mysql.noarch 0:5.5-1.3.amzn1
5
6 Dependency Installed:
7   mysql55.x86_64 0:5.5.24-1.24.amzn1                          mysql55-common.
         x86_64 0:5.5.24-1.24.amzn1
8
9 Complete!
10 $
```

2. Run commands that retrieve the secret and store them temporarily.

```
1 $ secret=$(aws secretsmanager get-secret-value --secret-id MyTestDatabaseMasterSecret | jq
      .SecretString | jq fromjson)
2 $ user=$(echo $secret | jq -r .username)
3 $ password=$(echo $secret | jq -r .password)
4 $ endpoint=$(echo $secret | jq -r .host)
5 $ port=$(echo $secret | jq -r .port)
```

The first command retrieves the secret from Secrets Manager. Then it pulls the `SecretString` field out of the JSON response and stores it in an environment variable. Each of the commands that follow parses out one additional credential piece or connection detail, and stores it in a separate environment variable.

3. Run a command that uses the parsed details to access your database.

```
1 $ mysql -h $endpoint -u $user -P $port -p$password
2 Warning: Using a password on the command line interface can be insecure.
3 Welcome to the MySQL monitor.  Commands end with ; or \g.
4 Your MySQL connection id is 44
5 Server version: 5.6.39 MySQL Community Server (GPL)
6
7 Copyright (c) 2000, 2018, Oracle and/or its affiliates. All rights reserved.
8
9 Oracle is a registered trademark of Oracle Corporation and/or its
10 affiliates. Other names may be trademarks of their respective
11 owners.
12
13 Type 'help;' or '\h' for help. Type '\c' to clear the current input statement.
14
15 mysql>
```

4. At the `mysql>` prompt, run a command that verifies your connection to the database by using the credentials from the secret. Ensure that the **Current user** in the output is the user that's specified in your secret.

```
1 mysql> status;
2 --------------
3 /apollo/env/envImprovement/bin/mysql_real  Ver 14.14 Distrib 5.6.39, for Linux (x86_64)
      using  EditLine wrapper
4
5 Connection id:          48
6 Current database:
7 Current user:           adminuser@192-168-1-1.example.com
8 SSL:                    Not in use
9 Current pager:          less
10 Using outfile:          ''
11 Using delimiter:        ;
12 Server version:         5.6.39 MySQL Community Server (GPL)
13 Protocol version:       10
14 Connection:             mytestdatabaseinstance.randomcharacters.region.rds.amazonaws.com
      via TCP/IP
15 Server characterset:    latin1
16 Db     characterset:    latin1
17 Client characterset:    utf8
18 Conn.  characterset:    utf8
19 TCP port:               3306
20 Uptime:                 2 hours 52 min 24 sec
21
```

```
22 Threads: 2  Questions: 15249  Slow queries: 0  Opens: 319  Flush tables: 1  Open tables: 80
        Queries per second avg: 1.474
23 --------------
```

5. Close the connection with the following command:

```
1 mysql> quit
2 Bye
```

## Step 4: Configure Rotation for Your Secret

Now that the initial credentials in your secret have been validated, you can configure and start your first rotation.

1. In the Secrets Manager console, choose the secret **MyTestDatabaseMasterSecret**.

2. On the secret details page, in the **Rotation configuration** section, choose **Edit rotation**.

3. On the **Edit rotation configuration** page, choose **Enable automatic rotation**.

4. For **Select rotation interval**, choose **30 days**.

5. Under **Select which secret will be used to perform the rotation**, choose **Use this secret**.

6. Choose **Save**. Secrets Manager begins to configure rotation for your secret, including creating the Lambda rotation function and attaching a role that enables Secrets Manager to invoke the function.

7. Stay on the browser page with the **Rotation is being configured** message, until it changes to **Your secret MyTestDatabaseMasterSecret has been successfully stored and secret rotation is enabled.**

## Step 5: Verify Successful Rotation

Now that you've rotated the secret, you can confirm that the new credentials in the secret work to connect with your database.

1. Run the commands that retrieve the secret and store them temporarily in environment variables.

```
1 $ secret=$(aws secretsmanager get-secret-value --secret-id MyTestDatabaseMasterSecret | jq
        .SecretString | jq fromjson)
2 $ user=$(echo $secret | jq -r .username)
3 $ password=$(echo $secret | jq -r .password)
4 $ endpoint=$(echo $secret | jq -r .host)
5 $ port=$(echo $secret | jq -r .port)
```

2. Using the same MySQL client that you installed previously, run the command that uses the parsed details to access your database.

```
1 $ mysql -h $endpoint -u $user -P $port -p$password
2 Warning: Using a password on the command line interface can be insecure.
3 Welcome to the MySQL monitor.  Commands end with ; or \g.
4 Your MySQL connection id is 44
5 Server version: 5.6.39 MySQL Community Server (GPL)
6
7 Copyright (c) 2000, 2018, Oracle and/or its affiliates. All rights reserved.
8
9 Oracle is a registered trademark of Oracle Corporation and/or its
10 affiliates. Other names may be trademarks of their respective
11 owners.
12
```

13 Type 'help;' or '\h' for help. Type '\c' to clear the current input statement.
14
15 mysql>

3. At the mysql> prompt, run a command that verifies your connection to the database by using the credentials from the secret.

```
1 mysql> status;
2 --------------
3 /apollo/env/envImprovement/bin/mysql_real  Ver 14.14 Distrib 5.6.39, for Linux (x86_64)
      using  EditLine wrapper
4
5 Connection id:          48
6 Current database:
7 Current user:           adminuser@192-168-1-1.example.com
8 SSL:                    Not in use
9 Current pager:          less
10 Using outfile:          ' '
11 Using delimiter:        ;
12 Server version:         5.6.39 MySQL Community Server (GPL)
13 Protocol version:       10
14 Connection:             mytestdatabaseinstance.randomcharacters.region.rds.amazonaws.com
      via TCP/IP
15 Server characterset:    latin1
16 Db      characterset:    latin1
17 Client characterset:    utf8
18 Conn.  characterset:    utf8
19 TCP port:               3306
20 Uptime:                 2 hours 52 min 24 sec
21
22 Threads: 2  Questions: 15249  Slow queries: 0  Opens: 319  Flush tables: 1  Open tables: 80
      Queries per second avg: 1.474
23 --------------
```

4. Ensure that the **Current user** in the output is the user that's specified in your secret.

5. Close the connection with the following command:

```
1 mysql> quit
2 Bye
```

# Step 6: Clean Up

**Important**
If you intend to also perform the tutorial Tutorial: Rotating a User Secret with a Master Secret, then don't perform these steps until you complete that tutorial as well.

Because databases and secrets can incur charges on your AWS bill, you should remove the database instance and the secret that you created in this tutorial after you're finished experimenting.

**To delete the secret**

1. Open the Secrets Manager console at https://console.aws.amazon.com/secretsmanager/.

2. In the list of secrets, choose the **MyTestDatabaseSecret** secret that you created for this tutorial.

3. Choose **Actions**, then choose **Delete secret**.

4. In the **Schedule secret deletion** dialog box, for **Enter a waiting period**, type **7**. This is the minimum value allowed.

5. Choose **Schedule deletion**.

   After the number of days in the recovery window elapses, Secrets Manager removes the secret permanently.

**To delete the database instance**

1. Open the Amazon RDS console at https://console.aws.amazon.com/rds/.

2. In the navigation pane, choose **Instances**.

3. In the list of available instances, choose the **MyTestDatabaseInstance** instance that you created for this tutorial.

4. Choose **Instance actions**, and then choose **Delete**.

5. On the **Delete DB Instance** page, in the **Options** section, for **Create final snapshot**, choose **No**.

6. Select the acknowledgement that all of your data will be lost, and then choose **Delete**.

# Tutorial: Rotating a User Secret with a Master Secret

This tutorial builds on what you completed in the first tutorial: Tutorial: Rotating a Secret for an AWS Database. It requires that you complete those steps first.

In this tutorial, you treat the secret that you already have as the master user for the database. You create a new limited user, and create a secret for that user. You then configure rotation for the user secret to work by using the credentials in the master secret. The Lambda rotation function for a master secret clones the first user, and then alternates between the users, changing the password for each in turn.

### Step 1: Create a New User for Your Database and a User Secret
First, you create a new limited-permissions user on your Amazon RDS MySQL database and store those credentials in a new secret.

### Step 2: Validate Your Initial Secret
In step 2, you confirm that you can access the database as your new user by using the credentials that are stored in the secret.

### Step 3: Configure Rotation for Your Secret
In step 3, you configure rotation for your user secret. You specify that the master secret should be used to grant access to the rotation function.

### Step 4: Verify Successful Rotation
In this step, we rotate the secret twice to show that the secret retrieves working credentials from two alternating users that can access the database.

### Step 5: Clean Up
In the final step, we remove the Amazon RDS database instance and the secrets that you created to avoid incurring any unnecessary costs.

## Prerequisites

- This tutorial assumes that you have access to an AWS account. It also assumes that you can sign in to AWS as a user with full permissions to operate AWS Secrets Manager and Amazon RDS, in either the console or by using the equivalent commands in the AWS CLI.
- You must have already completed the steps in the tutorial Tutorial: Rotating a Secret for an AWS Database, without deleting the database and user as described in the final section. That provides you with the following:
  - An Amazon RDS MySQL database called **MyTestDatabase** that's running in an instance called **MyTestDatabaseInstance**.
  - A master user named **adminuser** that has administrative permissions.
  - A secret named **MyTestDatabaseMasterSecret** that has the credentials for **adminuser** stored in it.

## Step 1: Create a New User for Your Database and a User Secret

From the original tutorial, you have an Amazon RDS MySQL database with a single admin *master* user. You also have a secret that can be queried to retrieve the latest credentials for that master user. In this step, you create a new, more-limited user and store its credentials in a secret. This secret could be used by, for example, a mobile app that needs to query information from the database. The user doesn't need anything other than read permissions, so it can't change its own password.

1. Open a command prompt where you can run the AWS CLI and your MySQL client (as installed in the previous tutorial). Run the following commands to retrieve the master secret. Then use the secret to sign in to the MySQL server.

```
1 $ secret=$(aws secretsmanager get-secret-value --secret-id MyTestDatabaseMasterSecret | jq
    .SecretString | jq fromjson)
2 $ user=$(echo $secret | jq -r .username)
3 $ password=$(echo $secret | jq -r .password)
4 $ endpoint=$(echo $secret | jq -r .host)
5 $ port=$(echo $secret | jq -r .port)
6 $ mysql -h $endpoint -u $user -P $port -p$password
```

2. Now run the following commands at the mysql> prompt to create a new, restricted-permissions user. Replace the sample password with one only you know, but remember it for the following steps.

```
1 mysql> CREATE USER mytestuser IDENTIFIED BY 'ReplaceThisWithASecurePassword';
2 Query OK, 0 rows affected (0.07 sec)
```

```
1 mysql> GRANT SELECT on *.* TO mytestuser;
2 Query OK, 0 rows affected (0.08 sec)
```

3. Open the Secrets Manager console at https://console.aws.amazon.com/secretsmanager/.

4. On the page with the list of secrets in your account, choose **Store a new secret**.

5. On the **Create Secret** page, in the **Select secret type** section, choose **Credentials for RDS database**.

6. For **User name**, type **mytestuser** to match the name of the user that you created in Step 1b.

7. For **Password**, type the same password that you provided for **mytestuser** in Step 1b.

8. For **Select the encryption key**, leave it set to **DefaultEncryptionKey**.

9. For **Select which RDS database this secret will access**, choose the instance **MyTestDatabaseInstance** that you created in the previous tutorial.

10. Choose **Next**.

11. In the **Secret name and description** section, for **Secret name** type **MyTestDatabaseUserSecret**.

12. In the **Configure automatic rotation** section, leave rotation disabled for now. Choose **Next**.

13. In the **Review** section, verify your details and then choose **Store**.

You're returned to the list of secrets, which now includes your new secret.

## Step 2: Validate Your Initial Secret

Before you configure your secret to rotate automatically, you should verify that the information in your secret is correct and can be used to connect to the database. In the previous tutorial, you installed a Linux-based MySQL client component. Continue to use that tool here.

If you're running this tutorial on some other platform, you might have to translate these commands into equivalents for your platform. At the very least, you can retrieve the secret by using either the AWS CLI or the Secrets Manager console. Cut and paste the user name and password into whatever MySQL database client you have.

1. Run commands that retrieve the secret and store them temporarily.

```
1 $ secret=$(aws secretsmanager get-secret-value --secret-id MyTestDatabaseUserSecret | jq .
    SecretString | jq fromjson)
2 $ user=$(echo $secret | jq -r .username)
3 $ password=$(echo $secret | jq -r .password)
4 $ endpoint=$(echo $secret | jq -r .host)
5 $ port=$(echo $secret | jq -r .port)
```

The first command retrieves the secret from Secrets Manager. Then it pulls the `SecretString` field out of the JSON response and stores it in an environment variable. Each of the commands that follow parses out one additional credential piece or connection detail, and stores it in a separate environment variable.

2. Run a command that uses the parsed details to access your database.

```
1 $ mysql -h $endpoint -u $user -P $port -p$password
2 Warning: Using a password on the command line interface can be insecure.
3 Welcome to the MySQL monitor.  Commands end with ; or \g.
4 Your MySQL connection id is 44
5 Server version: 5.6.39 MySQL Community Server (GPL)
6
7 Copyright (c) 2000, 2018, Oracle and/or its affiliates. All rights reserved.
8
9 Oracle is a registered trademark of Oracle Corporation and/or its
10 affiliates. Other names may be trademarks of their respective
11 owners.
12
13 Type 'help;' or '\h' for help. Type '\c' to clear the current input statement.
14
15 mysql>
```

3. At the `mysql>` prompt, run a command that verifies your connection to the database by using the credentials from the secret. Ensure that the **Current user** in the output is the user that's specified in your secret.

```
1 mysql> status;
2 --------------
3 /apollo/env/envImprovement/bin/mysql_real  Ver 14.14 Distrib 5.6.39, for Linux (x86_64)
       using  EditLine wrapper
4
5 Connection id:          48
6 Current database:
7 Current user:           mytestuser@192-168-1-1.example.com
8 SSL:                    Not in use
9 Current pager:          less
10 Using outfile:          ''
11 Using delimiter:        ;
12 Server version:         5.6.39 MySQL Community Server (GPL)
13 Protocol version:       10
14 Connection:             mytestdatabaseinstance.randomcharacters.region.rds.amazonaws.com
       via TCP/IP
15 Server characterset:    latin1
16 Db      characterset:    latin1
17 Client characterset:    utf8
18 Conn.   characterset:    utf8
19 TCP port:               3306
20 Uptime:                 2 hours 52 min 24 sec
21
22 Threads: 2  Questions: 15249  Slow queries: 0  Opens: 319  Flush tables: 1  Open tables: 80
       Queries per second avg: 1.474
23 --------------
```

4. Close the connection with the following command:

```
1 mysql> quit
2 Bye
```

31

## Step 3: Configure Rotation for Your Secret

Now that the initial credentials in your secret have been validated, you can configure and start your first rotation.

1. In the Secrets Manager console, choose the secret **MyTestDatabaseUserSecret**.

2. On the secret details page, in the **Rotation configuration** section, choose **Edit rotation**.

3. On the **Edit rotation configuration** page, choose **Enable automatic rotation**.

4. For **Select rotation interval**, choose **30 days**.

5. Under **Select which secret will be used to perform the rotation**, choose **Use a secret that I have previously stored in AWS Secrets Manager**.

6. In the list of secrets that appears, choose **MyTestDatabaseMasterSecret**.

7. Choose **Save**.

   Rotation configuration begins, but the initial rotation fails because of one step that you must (for security purposes) perform yourself.

8. When rotation configuration completes, the following message appears at the top of the page:

   *Your secret test/MyTestDatabaseUserSecret has been successfully stored and secret rotation is enabled. To finish configuring rotation, you need to provide the* role *permissions to access the value of the secret arn:aws:secretsmanager:us-east-1:123456789012MyTestDatabaseMasterSecret-QZhDKU.*

   You need to manually modify the policy for the role to grant the rotation function GetSecretValue access to the master secret. We can't do this for you for security reasons. Rotation of the secret continues to fail until you complete the following steps because the rotation policy doesn't have access to your master secret.

9. Copy the Amazon Resource Name (ARN) of the master secret from the message to your clipboard.

10. Choose the link on the word "role" in the message. This opens the role details page in the IAM console, for the role that's attached to the Lambda rotation function that Secrets Manager created for you.

11. On the **Permissions** tab, choose **Add inline policy**, and then set the following values:
    - For **Service**, choose **Secrets Manager**.
    - For **Actions**, choose **GetSecretValue**.
    - For **Resources**, choose **Add ARN** next to the **secret** resource type entry.
    - In the **Add ARN(s)** dialog box, paste the ARN of the master secret that you copied previously, and then choose **Add**.

12. Choose **Review policy**, and for **Name**, type **AccessToMasterSecret**.

13. Choose **Create policy**. **Note**
    As an alternative to using the Visual Editor as described in the previous steps, you can paste the following statement into an existing or new policy:

```
1 { "Effect": "Allow", "Action": [ "secretsmanager:GetSecretValue" ], "Resource": "<ARN of the
    master secret>" }
```

1. Return to the AWS Secrets Manager console.

2. On the **Secrets** list page, choose the name of your user secret.

3. Choose **Retrieve secret value** and view your current password. It's either the original password or a new one that's created by a successful rotation. If the original password is still there, close the **Secret value** section and reopen it until it successfully changes. It might take a few minutes. After it does change, move on to the next step.

## Step 4: Verify Successful Rotation

Now that you have rotated the secret, you can confirm that the new credentials in the secret work to connect with your database.

1. Run the commands that retrieve the secret, and store them temporarily in environment variables.

```
1 $ secret=$(aws secretsmanager get-secret-value --secret-id MyTestDatabaseUserSecret | jq .
     SecretString | jq fromjson)
2 $ user=$(echo $secret | jq -r .username)
3 $ password=$(echo $secret | jq -r .password)
4 $ endpoint=$(echo $secret | jq -r .host)
5 $ port=$(echo $secret | jq -r .port)
```

2. Using the same MySQL client that you installed previously, run the command that uses the parsed details to access your database.

```
1 $ mysql -h $endpoint -u $user -P $port -p$password
2 Warning: Using a password on the command line interface can be insecure.
3 Welcome to the MySQL monitor.  Commands end with ; or \g.
4 Your MySQL connection id is 44
5 Server version: 5.6.39 MySQL Community Server (GPL)
6
7 Copyright (c) 2000, 2018, Oracle and/or its affiliates. All rights reserved.
8
9 Oracle is a registered trademark of Oracle Corporation and/or its
10 affiliates. Other names may be trademarks of their respective
11 owners.
12
13 Type 'help;' or '\h' for help. Type '\c' to clear the current input statement.
14
15 mysql>
```

3. At the mysql> prompt, run a command that verifies your connection to the database by using the credentials from the secret. Check that the **Current user** in the output is either the user that's specified in your first user secret, or that same user name suffixed with "_clone". This shows that the rotation has successfully cloned your original nuser and alternated it in a new version of the secret.

```
1 mysql> status;
2 --------------
3 /apollo/env/envImprovement/bin/mysql_real  Ver 14.14 Distrib 5.6.39, for Linux (x86_64)
       using  EditLine wrapper
4
5 Connection id:          48
6 Current database:
7 Current user:           mytestuser_clone@192-168-1-1.example.com
8 SSL:                    Not in use
9 Current pager:          less
10 Using outfile:          ''
11 Using delimiter:        ;
12 Server version:         5.6.39 MySQL Community Server (GPL)
13 Protocol version:       10
14 Connection:             mytestdatabaseinstance.randomcharacters.region.rds.amazonaws.com
       via TCP/IP
15 Server characterset:    latin1
16 Db      characterset:   latin1
17 Client characterset:    utf8
```

33

```
18 Conn.  characterset:    utf8
19 TCP port:               3306
20 Uptime:                 2 hours 52 min 24 sec
21
22 Threads: 2  Questions: 15249  Slow queries: 0  Opens: 319  Flush tables: 1  Open tables: 80
        Queries per second avg: 1.474
23 --------------
```

4. Close the connection with the following command:

```
1 mysql> quit
2 Bye
```

## Step 5: Clean Up

Because databases and secrets can incur charges on your AWS bill, you should remove the database instance and the secret that you created in this tutorial.

**To delete the secret**

1. Open the Secrets Manager console at https://console.aws.amazon.com/secretsmanager/.

2. In the list of secrets, choose the **MyTestDatabaseSecret** secret that you created for this tutorial.

3. Choose **Actions**, and then choose **Delete secret**.

4. In the **Schedule secret deletion** dialog box, for **Enter a waiting period**, type **7**. This is the minimum value allowed.

5. Choose **Schedule deletion**.

   After the number of days in the recovery window elapses, Secrets Manager removes the secret permanently.

**To delete the database instance**

1. Open the Amazon RDS console at https://console.aws.amazon.com/rds/.

2. In the navigation pane, choose **Instances**.

3. In the list of available instances, choose the **MyTestDatabaseInstance** instance that you created for this tutorial.

4. Choose **Instance actions**, and then choose **Delete**.

5. On the **Delete DB Instance** page, in the **Options** section, for **Create final snapshot**, choose **No**.

6. Select the acknowledgement that all of your data will be lost, and then choose **Delete**.

# AWS Secrets Manager Best Practices

The following recommendations help you to more securely use AWS Secrets Manager:

**Topics**

- Protect Additional Sensitive Information
- Mitigate the Risks of Logging and Debugging Your Lambda Function
- Mitigate the Risks of Using the AWS CLI to Store Your Secrets

## Protect Additional Sensitive Information

A secret often includes several pieces of information beyond the user name and password. Depending on the database, service, or website, you can choose to include additional sensitive data. This data can include password hints, or question-and-answer pairs that you can use to recover your password if you forgot it.

Make sure that any information that might be used to gain access to the credentials in the secret is protected as securely as the credentials themselves. Don't store such information in the `Description` or any other non-encrypted part of the secret.

Instead, store all such sensitive information as part of the encrypted secret value (in either the `SecretString` or `SecretBinary` field). You can store up to 4096 characters in the secret. In the `SecretString` field, the text usually takes the form of JSON key-value string pairs, as shown in the following example:

```
1 {
2     "username": "saanvisarkar",
3     "password": "i29wwX!%9wFV",
4     "host": "http://myserver.example.com",
5     "port": "1234",
6     "database": "myDatabase"
7 }
```

## Mitigate the Risks of Logging and Debugging Your Lambda Function

When you create a custom Lambda rotation function to support your Secrets Manager secret, be careful about including debugging or logging statements in your function. These statements can cause information in your function to be written to CloudWatch. Ensure that this logging of information to CloudWatch doesn't include any of the sensitive data that's stored in the encrypted secret value. Also, if you do choose to include any such statements in your code during development for testing and debugging purposes, make sure that you remove those lines from the code before it's used in production. Also, remember to remove any logs that include sensitive information that was collected during development after it's no longer needed.

These kinds of logging and debug statements aren't included in any of the Lambda functions that AWS provides for supported databases.

## Mitigate the Risks of Using the AWS CLI to Store Your Secrets

When you use the AWS Command Line Interface (AWS CLI) to invoke AWS operations, you enter those commands in a command shell. For example, you can use the Windows command prompt or Windows PowerShell, or the Bash or Z shell, among others. Many of these command shells include functionality that's designed to increase productivity. But this functionality could be used to compromise your secrets. For example, in most shells, you can use the up arrow key to see the last command that was entered. This *command history* feature could be exploited by anyone who walks up to your unsecured session. Also, other utilities that work in the background might have access to your command parameters (with the intended goal of helping you get your tasks done more efficiently). To mitigate such risks, ensure that you take the following steps:

- Always lock your computer when you walk away from your console.

- Uninstall or disable console utilities that you don't need or no longer use.

- Ensure that both the shell and the remote access program (if you are using one) don't log the commands you type.

- Use techniques to pass parameters that aren't captured by shell's command history. The following example shows how you can type the secret text into a text file, which is then passed to the AWS Secrets Manager command and immediately destroyed. This means that the secret text isn't captured by the typical shell history.

  The following example shows typical Linux commands (your shell might require slightly different commands):

```
1 $ touch secret.txt
                                                          # Creates an
    empty text file
2 $ chmod go-rx secret.txt
                                                        # Restricts access
    to the file to only the user
3 $ cat > secret.txt
                                                          # Redirects
    standard input (STDIN) to the text file
4 ThisIsMyTopSecretPassword^Z
                                                            # Everything the user
    types from this point up to the CTRL-Z (^Z) is saved in the file
5 $ aws secretsmanager create-secret --name TestSecret --secret-string file://secret.txt
            # The Secrets Manager command takes the --secret-string parameter from the
    contents of the file
6 $ shred -u secret.txt
                                                          # The file is
    destroyed so it can no longer be accessed.
```

After you run these commands, you should be able to use the up and down arrows to scroll through the command history and see that the secret text isn't displayed on any line.

**Important**
By default, you can't perform an equivalent technique in Windows unless you first reduce the size of the command history buffer to **1**.

**To configure the Windows Command Prompt to have only 1 command history buffer of 1 command**

1. Open an Administrator command prompt (**Run as administrator**).

2. Choose the icon in the upper left on the title bar, and then choose **Properties**.

3. On the **Options** tab, set **Buffer Size** and **Number of Buffers** both to **1**, and then choose **OK**.

4. Whenever you have to type a command that you don't want in the history, immediately follow it with one other command, such as:

```
1 echo.
```

   This ensures that the sensitive command is flushed.

For the Windows Command Prompt shell, you can download the SysInternals SDelete tool, and then use commands that are similar to the following:

```
1 C:\> echo. 2> secret.txt                                                            #
     Creates an empty file
2 C:\> icacls secret.txt /remove "BUILTIN\Administrators" "NT AUTHORITY/SYSTEM" /inheritance:r   #
     Restricts access to the file to only the owner
3 C:\> copy con secret.txt /y                                                         #
     Redirects the keyboard to text file, suppressing prompt to overwrite
4 THIS IS MY TOP SECRET PASSWORD^Z                                                    #
     Everything the user types from this point up to the CTRL-Z (^Z) is saved in the file
5 C:\> aws secretsmanager create-secret --name TestSecret --secret-string file://secret.txt   #
     The Secrets Manager command takes the --secret-string parameter from the contents of the
     file
6 C:\> sdelete secret.txt                                                             #
     The file is destroyed so it can no longer be accessed.
```

# Creating and Managing Secrets with AWS Secrets Manager

In this section, we describe how to create, update, and retrieve secrets by using AWS Secrets Manager.

**Topics**

- Creating a Basic Secret
- Modifying a Secret
- Retrieving the Secret Value
- Deleting and Restoring a Secret

# Creating a Basic Secret

AWS Secrets Manager enables you to store basic secrets with a minimum of effort. A "basic" secret is one with a minimum of metadata and a single encrypted secret value. The one version that's stored in the secret is automatically labeled `AWSCURRENT`.

**To create a basic secret**
Follow the steps under one of the following tabs:

---

[ **Using the console** ]

**Minimum permissions**
To create a secret in the console, you must have these permissions:
The permissions granted by the **SecretsManagerReadWrite** AWS managed policy. The permissions granted by the **IAMFullAccess** AWS managed policy – required only if you need to enable rotation for the secret. `kms:CreateKey` – required only if you need to ask Secrets Manager to create a custom AWS KMS customer master key (CMK). `kms:Encrypt` – required only if you use a custom AWS KMS key to encrypt your secret instead of the default Secrets Manager CMK for your account.

1. Sign in to the AWS Secrets Manager console at https://console.aws.amazon.com/secretsmanager/.

2. Choose **Store a new secret**.

3. In the **Select secret type** section, specify the kind of secret that you want to create by choosing one of the following options. Then supply the required information.

---

[ **Credentials for Amazon RDS database** ]

This secret is for one of the supported database services for which Secrets Manager provides full rotation support with a preconfigured Lambda rotation function. You need specify only the authentication credentials because Secrets Manager learns everything else it needs by querying the database instance.

1. Type the user name and password that allow access to the database. Choose a user that has only the permissions that are required by the customer who will access this secret.

2. Choose the AWS KMS encryption key that you want to use to encrypt the protected text in the secret. If you don't choose one, Secrets Manager checks to see if there's a default key for the account, and uses it if it exists. If a default key doesn't exist, Secrets Manager creates one for you automatically. You can also choose **Add new key** to create a custom CMK specifically for this secret. To create your own AWS KMS CMK, you must have permissions to create CMKs in your account.

3. Choose the database instance from the list. Secrets Manager retrieves the connection details about the database by querying the chosen instance.

---

[ **Credentials for other database** ]

This secret is for a database service that Secrets Manager knows about and supports. However, Secrets Manager needs you to provide additional information about the database. To rotate this secret, you must write a custom Lambda rotation function that can parse the secret and interact with the service to rotate the secret on your behalf.

1. Type the user name and password that allow access to the database that you want to protect in this secret.

2. Choose the AWS KMS encryption key that you want to use to encrypt the protected text in the secret. If you don't choose one, Secrets Manager checks to see if there's a default key for the account, and uses it if it exists. If a default key doesn't exist, Secrets Manager creates one for you automatically. You can also choose **Add new key** to create a custom CMK specifically for this secret. To create your own AWS KMS CMK, you must have permissions to create CMKs in your account.

3. Choose the type of database engine that runs your database.

4. Specify the connection details by typing the database server's IP address, database name, and TCP port number.

---

**[ Other type of secret ]**

This secret is for a database or service that Secrets Manager doesn't natively know about. You must supply the structure and details of your secret. To rotate this secret, you must write a custom Lambda rotation function that can parse the secret and interact with the service to rotate the secret on your behalf.

1. Specify the details of your custom secret as **Key** and **Value** pairs. For example, you can specify a key of UserName, and then supply the appropriate user name as its value. Add a second key with the name of Password and the password text as its value. You could also add entries for Database name, Server address, TCP port, and so on. You can add as many pairs as you need to store the information you require.

   Alternatively, you can choose the **Plaintext** tab and enter the secret value in any way you like.

2. Choose the AWS KMS encryption key that you want to use to encrypt the protected text in the secret. If you don't choose one, Secrets Manager checks to see if there's a default key for the account, and uses it if it exists. If a default key doesn't exist, Secrets Manager creates one for you automatically. You can also choose **Add new key** to create a custom CMK specifically for this secret. To create your own AWS KMS CMK, you must have permissions to create CMKs in your account.

---

1. For **Secret name**, type an optional path and name, such as **production/MyAwesomeAppSecret** or **development/TestSecret**. You can optionally add a description to help you remember the purpose of this secret later on.

   The secret name must be ASCII letters, digits, or any of the following characters : /_+=,.@-

2. (Optional) At this point, you can configure rotation for your secret. Because we're working on a "basic" secret without rotation, leave it at **Disable automatic rotation**, and then choose **Next**.

   For information about how to configure rotation on new or existing secrets, see Rotating Your AWS Secrets Manager Secrets.

3. Review your settings, and then choose **Store secret** to save everything you entered as a new secret in Secrets Manager.

---

**[ Using the AWS CLI or AWS SDK operations ]**

You can use the following commands to create a basic secret in Secrets Manager:

- **API/SDK:** http://docs.aws.amazon.com/secretsmanager/latest/apireference/API_CreateSecret.html
- **AWS CLI:** http://docs.aws.amazon.com/cli/latest/reference/secretsmanager/create-secret.html

**Example**

Here's an example AWS CLI command that performs the equivalent of the console-based secret creation on the other tab. This command assumes that you've placed your secret, such as this example JSON text structure {"username":"anika","password":"aDM4N3*!8TT"}, in a file named mycreds.json.

```
1 $ aws secretsmanager create-secret --name production/MyAwesomeAppSecret --secret-string file://
    mycreds.json
2 {
3     "SecretARN": "arn:aws:secretsmanager:region:accountid:secret:production/MyAwesomeAppSecret-
        AbCdEf",
4     "SecretName": "production/MyAwesomeAppSecret",
5     "SecretVersionId": "EXAMPLE1-90ab-cdef-fedc-ba987EXAMPLE"
6 }
```

The ClientRequestToken parameter isn't required because we're using the AWS CLI, which automatically generates and supplies one for us. We also don't need the KmsKeyId parameter because we're using the default Secrets Manager CMK for the account. If you're using SecretString, you can't use SecretBinary. SecretType is reserved for use by the Secrets Manager console.

In a working environment, where your customers use an app that uses the secret to access a database, you might still need to grant permissions to the IAM user or role that the app uses to access the secret. You can attach a policy to the user or role that identifies that identifies the secret in the Resource element.

---

# Modifying a Secret

You can modify some elements of a secret after you create it. In the console, you can edit the description, edit or attach a new resource-based policy to modify permissions to the secret, change the AWS KMS customer master key (CMK) that's used to encrypt and decrypt the protected secret information, and edit or add or remove tags.

You can also change the value of the encrypted secret information. However, we recommend that you use rotation to update secret values that contain credentials. Rotation doesn't just update the secret. It also modifies the credentials on the protected database or service to match those in the secret. This keeps them automatically synchronized so that when clients request a secret value, they always retrieve a working set of credentials.

This section includes procedures and commands that describe how to modify the following elements of a secret:

- Encrypted secret value
- Description
- AWS KMS encryption key
- Tags

**To modify the encrypted secret value stored in a secret**
Follow the steps under one of the following tabs:

**Important**
Updating the secret in this manner doesn't change the credentials on the protected server. If you want the credentials on the server to stay in sync with the credentials stored in the secret value, we recommend that you enable rotation. An AWS Lambda function changes both the credentials on the server and those in the secret to match, and tests that the updated credentials work. For more information, see Rotating Your AWS Secrets Manager Secrets.

---

[ **Using the console** ]

When you update the encrypted secret value in a secret, you create a new version of the secret. The new version automatically gets the staging label `AWSCURRENT` moved to it. The old version is still accessible by querying for the staging label `AWSPREVIOUS`. This isn't the same as rotation.

**Note**
Any time the staging label `AWSCURRENT` moves from one version to another, Secrets Manager automatically moves the staging label `AWSPREVIOUS` to the version that `AWSCURRENT` was just removed from.

1. Open the Secrets Manager console at https://console.aws.amazon.com/secretsmanager/.

2. In the list of secrets, choose the name of the secret with the secret value that you want to modify.

3. In the **Secret value** section, choose **Retrieve secret value**.

4. With the secret value now displayed, choose `Edit`.

5. Update the values as appropriate, and then choose **Save**.

---

[ **Using the AWS CLI or AWS SDK operations** ]

You can use the following commands to update the encrypted secret value that's stored in the secret. When you update the encrypted secret value in a secret, you create a new version of the secret.

**Note**
`UpdateSecret` automatically moves the staging label `AWSCURRENT` to the new version of the secret.
`PutSecretValue` *does not* automatically move staging labels. However, it does add `AWSCURRENT` if this command creates the first version of the secret. Otherwise, it only attaches or moves those labels that you explicitly request

with the `VersionStages` parameter.

Any time the staging label `AWSCURRENT` moves from one version to another, Secrets Manager automatically moves the staging label `AWSPREVIOUS` to the version that `AWSCURRENT` was just removed from.

- **API/SDK:** http://docs.aws.amazon.com/secretsmanager/latest/apireference/API_UpdateSecret, http://docs.aws.amazon.com/secretsmanager/latest/apireference/API_PutSecretValue.html
- **AWS CLI:** http://docs.aws.amazon.com/cli/latest/reference/secretsmanager/update-secret.html, http://docs.aws.amazon.com/cli/latest/reference/secretsmanager/put-secret-value.html

**Example**

The following example AWS CLI command changes the secret value for a secret. This results in the creation of a new version. Secrets Manager automatically moves the `AWSCURRENT` staging label to the new version. Also, the `AWSPREVIOUS` staging label is automatically moved to the older version that `AWSCURRENT` was just removed from.

```
1 $ aws secretsmanager update-secret --secret-id production/MyAwesomeAppSecret --secret-string '{"
    username":"anika","password":"a different password"}'
2 {
3     "SecretARN": "arn:aws:secretsmanager:us-west-2:123456789012:secret:production/
        MyAwesomeAppSecret-AbCdEf",
4     "SecretName": "production/MyAwesomeAppSecret",
5     "SecretVersionId": "EXAMPLE1-90ab-cdef-fedc-ba987EXAMPLE"
6 }
```

The `SecretVersionId` in the output is the unique secret version ID of the new version of the secret. You can manually provide the value by using the `ClientRequestToken` parameter. If you don't specify the value, the SDK or AWS CLI generates a random UUID value for you.

------

**To modify the description of a secret**

Follow the steps under one of the following tabs:

---

[ **Using the console** ]

1. Open the Secrets Manager console at https://console.aws.amazon.com/secretsmanager/.

2. In the list of secrets, choose the name of the secret that you want to modify.

3. In the **Secrets details** section, choose **Actions**, and then choose **Edit description**.

4. Type a new description or edit the existing text, and then choose **Save**.

---

[ **Using the AWS CLI or AWS SDK operations** ]

You can use the following commands to modify the description of a secret in AWS Secrets Manager:

- **API/SDK:** http://docs.aws.amazon.com/secretsmanager/latest/apireference/API_UpdateSecret.html
- **AWS CLI:** http://docs.aws.amazon.com/cli/latest/reference/secretsmanager/update-secret.html

**Example**

The following example AWS CLI command adds or replaces the description with the one provided by the `--description` parameter.

```
1 $ aws secretsmanager update-secret --secret-id production/MyAwesomeAppSecret --description 'This
    is the description I want to attach to the secret.'
2 {
```

```
3      "SecretARN": "arn:aws:secretsmanager:region:accountid:secret:production/MyAwesomeAppSecret-
          AbCdEf",
4      "SecretName": "production/MyAwesomeAppSecret",
5      "SecretVersionId": "EXAMPLE1-90ab-cdef-fedc-ba987EXAMPLE"
6  }
```

------

**To modify the AWS KMS encryption key used by a secret**

Follow the steps under one of the following tabs:

---

**[ Using the console ]**

**Important**

If you change the encryption key that's used by a secret, old versions of the secret are no longer accessible. This is because the new key can't decrypt secret values for the older versions. If you change the encryption key that's used by a secret, you must update the secret value (with UpdateSecret or PutSecretValue) at least once before you disable or delete the first CMK. Updating the secret value decrypts it using the old CMK and reencrypts it with the new CMK. If you disable or delete the first CMK before this update, the key cannot be decrypted and you lose the contents of the secret unless you can re-enable the CMK.

1. Open the Secrets Manager console at https://console.aws.amazon.com/secretsmanager/.

2. In the list of secrets, choose the name of the secret that you want to modify.

3. In the **Secrets details** section, choose **Actions**, and then choose **Edit encryption key**.

4. Choose the AWS KMS encryption key that you want to use to encrypt and decrypt later versions of your secret. Then choose **Save**.

---

**[ Using the AWS CLI or AWS SDK operations ]**

**Important**

If you change the encryption key that's used by a secret, old versions of the secret are no longer accessible. This is because the new key can't decrypt secret values for the older versions. If you change the encryption key that's used by a secret, you must update the secret value (with UpdateSecret or PutSecretValue) at least once before you disable or delete the first CMK. Updating the secret value decrypts it using the old CMK and reencrypts it with the new CMK. If you disable or delete the first CMK before this update, the key cannot be decrypted and you lose the contents of the secret unless you can re-enable the CMK.

You can use the following commands to modify the AWS KMS encryption key that's used by the secret. You must specify the CMK by its Amazon Resource Name (ARN).

- **API/SDK:** http://docs.aws.amazon.com/secretsmanager/latest/apireference/API_UpdateSecret.html
- **AWS CLI:** http://docs.aws.amazon.com/cli/latest/reference/secretsmanager/update-secret.html

**Example**

The following example AWS CLI command adds or replaces the AWS KMS CMK that's used for all encryption and decryption operations in this secret from this time on.

```
1  $ aws secretsmanager update-secret --secret-id production/MyAwesomeAppSecret --kms-key-id arn:
      aws:kms:region:123456789012:key/EXAMPLE1-90ab-cdef-fedc-ba987EXAMPLE
```

------

**To modify the tags attached to a secret**

Follow the steps under one of the following tabs:

44

## [ Using the AWS CLI or AWS SDK operations ]

You can use the following commands to add or remove the tags that are attached to a secret in AWS Secrets Manager. Key names and values are case sensitive. Only one tag on a secret can have a given key name. To edit an existing tag, add a tag with the same key name. It doesn't add a new key-value pair. Instead, it updates the value in the existing pair. To change a key name, you must remove the first key and add a second with the new name.

- **API/SDK:** http://docs.aws.amazon.com/secretsmanager/latest/apireference/API_TagResource, http://docs.aws.amazon.com/secretsmanager/latest/apireference/API_UntagResource.html
- **AWS CLI:** http://docs.aws.amazon.com/cli/latest/reference/secretsmanager/tag-resource.html, http://docs.aws.amazon.com/cli/latest/reference/secretsmanager/untag-resource.html

### Example

The following example AWS CLI command adds or replaces the tags with those provided by the `--tags` parameter. The parameter is expected to be a JSON array of `Key` and `Value` elements:

```
1 $ aws secretsmanager tag-resource --secret-id MySecret2 --tags '[{"Key":"costcenter","Value":"12345"},{"Key":"environment","Value":"production"}]'
```

The tag-resource command doesn't return any output.

### Example

The following example AWS CLI command removes the tags with the key "environment" from the specified secret:

```
1 $ aws secretsmanager untag-resource --secret-id MySecret2 --tag-keys 'environment'
```

The tag-resource command doesn't return any output.

# Retrieving the Secret Value

One of the main purposes of Secrets Manager is to enable you to programmatically and securely retrieve your secrets in your custom applications. However, you can also retrieve them by using the console or the CLI tools.

This section includes procedures and commands that describe how to retrieve the secret value of a secret.

**To retrieve a secret value**
Follow the steps under one of the following tabs:

---

[ **Using the console** ]

## Minimum permissions

To retrieve a secret in the console, you must have these permissions:
`secretsmanager:ListSecrets` – Used to navigate to the secret you want to retrieve. `secretsmanager:DescribeSecret` — to retrieve the non-encrypted parts of the secret `secretsmanager:GetSecretValue` – Used to retrieve the encrypted part of the secret. `kms:Decrypt` – This is required only if you used a custom AWS KMS customer master key (CMK) to encrypt your secret.

1. Open the Secrets Manager console at https://console.aws.amazon.com/secretsmanager/.

2. In the list of secrets in your account, choose the name of the secret that you want to view.

   The **Secret details** page appears. It displays all of the chosen secret's configuration details except for the encrypted secret text.

3. In the **Credential data** section, choose **Retrieve credentials**.

4. Choose **secret key : secret value** to see the credentials parsed out as individual keys and values. Choose **Plaintext** to see the original JSON text string that's encrypted and stored.

---

[ **Using the AWS CLI or AWS SDK operations** ]

For more information about retrieving a secret from your application's code, see Retrieving the Secret Value.

You can use the following commands to retrieve a secret stored in AWS Secrets Manager:

- **API/SDK:** http://docs.aws.amazon.com/secretsmanager/latest/apireference/API_GetSecretValue.html
- **AWS CLI:** http://docs.aws.amazon.com/cli/latest/reference/secretsmanager/get-secret-value.html

You must identify the secret by its friendly name or Amazon Resource Name (ARN), and specify the version of the secret to return. (It defaults to the version that has the staging label `AWSCURRENT` if you don't otherwise specify a version). The contents of the secret text are returned in the response parameters `PlaintextString` and, if you stored any binary data in the secret, `Plaintext`, which returns a byte array.

## Example
The following example of the AWS CLI command decrypts and retrieves the encrypted secret information from the default version of the secret named "MyTestDatabase".

```
1 $ aws secretsmanager get-secret-value --secret-id development/MyTestDatabase
2 {
3     "SecretARN": "arn:aws:secretsmanager:region:accountid:secret:development/MyTestDatabase-
        AbCdEf",
4     "SecretName": "development/MyTestDatabase",
5     "SecretVersionId": "EXAMPLE1-90ab-cdef-fedc-ba987EXAMPLE",
6     "SecretString": "{\"ServerName\":\"MyDBServer\",\"UserName\":\"Anaya\",\"Password\":\"
        MyT0pSecretP@ssw0rd\"}",
```

```
 7      "SecretVersionStages": [
 8          "AWSCURRENT"
 9      ],
10      "CreatedDate": 1510089380.309
11  }
```

_____

# Deleting and Restoring a Secret

Because of the critical nature of secrets, AWS Secrets Manager intentionally makes deleting a secret a difficult thing to do. Secrets can't be *immediately* deleted. Instead, they're immediately made inaccessible and scheduled for deletion after a recovery window of a *minimum* of seven days. Until the recovery window ends, you can recover a secret that you previously deleted.

You also can't *directly* delete a version of a secret. Instead, you remove all staging labels from the secret. This marks the secret as deprecated, and enables Secrets Manager to automatically delete the version in the background.

This section includes procedures and commands that describe how to delete a secret and how to restore a deleted secret:

- Delete a secret with all of its versions
- Restore a secret that's scheduled for deletion
- Delete a version of a secret

**To delete a secret and all of its versions**
Follow the steps under one of the following tabs:

---

**[ Using the console ]**

When you delete a secret, it's immediately deprecated. However, it's not actually deleted until the number of days specified in the recovery window has gone by. A deprecated secret can't be accessed. If you have to access a secret that has been scheduled for deletion, you must restore the secret. Then you can access the secret and its encrypted secret information.

**Minimum permissions**
To delete a secret in the console, you must have these permissions:
`secretsmanager:ListSecrets` – Used to navigate to the secret that you want to delete. `secretsmanager:DeleteSecret` – Used to deprecate the secret and schedule it for permanent deletion.

1. Open the Secrets Manager console at https://console.aws.amazon.com/secretsmanager/.

2. Navigate to the list of secrets that you currently manage in Secrets Manager, and choose the name of the secret that you want to delete.

3. In the **Secret details** section, choose **Delete secret**.

4. In the **Schedule secret deletion** dialog box, specify the number of days in the recovery window. This represents the number of days that you want to wait before the deletion is permanent. Secrets Manager attaches a field called `DeletionDate` and sets it to the current date and time, plus the number of days that are specified for the recovery window.

5. Choose **Schedule deletion**.

6. If the option to show deleted items is enabled in the console, then the secret continues to display. You can optionally choose to view the **Deleted date** field in the list.

    1. Choose the **Preferences** icon (the gear ⚙) in the upper-right corner.

    2. Choose **Show secrets scheduled for deletion**.

    3. Enable the switch for **Deleted on**.

    4. Choose **Save**.

   Your deleted secrets now appear in the list, with the date on which you deleted each one.

## [ Using the AWS CLI or AWS SDK operations ]

You can use the following commands to retrieve a secret that's stored in AWS Secrets Manager:

- **API/SDK:** http://docs.aws.amazon.com/secretsmanager/latest/apireference/API_DeleteSecret.html
- **AWS CLI:** http://docs.aws.amazon.com/cli/latest/reference/secretsmanager/delete-secret.html

You have to identify the secret that you want to delete by its friendly name or Amazon Resource Name (ARN) in the `SecretId` field.

### Example
The following example of the AWS CLI command deprecates the secret named "MyTestDatabase" and schedules it to be deleted after a recovery window of 14 days.

```
1 $ aws secretsmanager delete-secret --secret-id development/MyTestDatabase --recovery-window-in-
    days 14
2 {
3     "SecretARN": "arn:aws:secretsmanager:region:accountid:secret:development/MyTestDatabase-
        AbCdEf",
4     "SecretName": "development/MyTestDatabase",
5     "DeletionDate": 1510089380.309
6 }
```

At any time after the date and time that are specified in the `DeletionDate` field, AWS Secrets Manager permanently deletes the secret.

------

### To restore a secret that's scheduled for deletion
Follow the steps under one of the following tabs:

---

## [ Using the console ]

A secret that's scheduled for deletion is considered deprecated and can no longer be directly accessed. After the recovery window has passed, Secrets Manager deletes the secret permanently. After the secret is deleted, it's not recoverable. Before the end of the recovery window, you can recover the secret and make it accessible again. This removes the `DeletionDate` field, which cancels the scheduled permanent deletion.

### Minimum permissions
To restore a secret and its metadata in the console, you must have these permissions:
`secretsmanager:ListSecrets` – Use to navigate to the secret that you want to restore. `secretsmanager:RestoreSecret` – Use to delete any versions that are still associated with the secret.

1. Open the Secrets Manager console at https://console.aws.amazon.com/secretsmanager/.

2. Navigate to the list of secrets that you currently manage in Secrets Manager.

3. To view deleted secrets, you must enable this ability in the console. If it's not already enabled, perform these steps:

4.

5. Choose the **Preferences** icon (the gear ⚙) in the upper-right corner.

6. Choose **Show secrets scheduled for deletion**.

7. Enable the switch for **Deleted on**.

8. Choose **Save**.

Your deleted secrets now appear in the list with the date on which you deleted each one.

1. Choose the name of the deleted secret that you want to restore.

2. In the **Secret details** section, choose **Cancel deletion**.

3. In the **Cancel secret deletion** confirmation dialog box, choose **Cancel deletion**.

   AWS Secrets Manager removes the `DeletionDate` field from the secret. This cancels the scheduled deletion and restores access to the secret.

---

### [ Using the AWS CLI or AWS SDK operations ]

You can use the following commands to retrieve a secret that's stored in AWS Secrets Manager:

- **API/SDK:** http://docs.aws.amazon.com/secretsmanager/latest/apireference/API_RestoreSecret.html
- **AWS CLI:** http://docs.aws.amazon.com/cli/latest/reference/secretsmanager/restore-secret.html

You must identify the secret that you want to restore by its friendly name or ARN in the `SecretId` field.

**Example**

The following example of the AWS CLI command restores a previously deleted secret named "MyTestDatabase". This cancels the scheduled deletion and restores access to the secret.

```
1 $ aws secretsmanager restore-secret --secret-id development/MyTestDatabase
2 {
3     "SecretARN": "arn:aws:secretsmanager:region:accountid:secret:development/MyTestDatabase-
        AbCdEf",
4     "SecretName": "development/MyTestDatabase"
5 }
```

------

### To delete one version of a secret
Follow the steps under one of the following tabs:

---

### [ Using the AWS CLI or AWS SDK operations ]

You can't delete one version of a secret using the Secrets Manager console. You must use the AWS CLI or AWS API.

You can't directly delete a version of a secret. Instead, you remove all its staging labels, which effectively marks it as deprecated. Secrets Manager can then delete it in the background.

You can use the following commands to deprecate a version of a secret that's stored in AWS Secrets Manager:

- **API/SDK:** http://docs.aws.amazon.com/secretsmanager/latest/apireference/API_GetSecretValue.html
- **AWS CLI:** http://docs.aws.amazon.com/cli/latest/reference/secretsmanager/get-secret-value.html

You must identify the secret by its friendly name or ARN. You also specify the staging labels that you want to add, move, or remove.

You can specify `FromSecretVersionId` and `MoveToSecretId` in the following combinations:

- `FromSecretVersionId` only: This deletes staging labels completely from the specified version. If the specified staging label isn't present on that version, then an error occurs.

- `MoveToVerionId` only: This adds the staging labels to the specified version. If any of the staging labels are already attached other versions, they are automatically removed from those versions.
- `MoveToVersionId` and `RemoveFromVersionId`: These explicitly move a label. The staging label must already be present on the `RemoveFromVersionId` version of the secret, or an error occurs.

**Example**

The following example of the AWS CLI command removes the `AWSPREVIOUS` staging label from a version of the secret named "MyTestDatabase". You can retrieve the version ID of the version you want to delete by using the [ListSecretVersionIds](AWS Secrets Manager API ReferenceAPI_ListSecretVersionIds.html) command.

```
1 $ aws secretsmanager update-secret-version-stage \
2         --secret-id development/MyTestDatabase \
3         --from-secret-version-id EXAMPLE1-90ab-cdef-fedc-ba987EXAMPLE
4         --secret-version-stage AWSPREVIOUS
5 {
6     "ARN": "arn:aws:secretsmanager:region:accountid:secret:development/MyTestDatabase-AbCdEf",
7     "Name": "development/MyTestDatabase"
8 }
```

---

# Rotating Your AWS Secrets Manager Secrets

You can configure AWS Secrets Manager to automatically rotate the secret for a secured service or database. Secrets Manager already natively knows how to rotate secrets for supported Amazon RDS databases. However, Secrets Manager also can enable you to rotate secrets for other databases or third-party services. Because each service or database can have a unique way of configuring its secrets, Secrets Manager uses a Lambda function that you can customize to work with whatever database or service that you choose. You customize the Lambda function to implement the service-specific details of how to rotate a secret.

When you enable rotation for a secret by using the **Credentials for RDS database** secret type, Secrets Manager provides a Lambda rotation function for you and populates the function's Amazon Resource Name (ARN) in the secret automatically. You typically don't need to do anything for this to work other than to provide a few details. For example, you specify which secret has permissions to rotate the credentials, and how often you want to rotate the secret.

When you enable rotation for a secret with **Credentials for other database** or some **Other type of secret**, you must provide the code for the Lambda function. The code includes the commands that are required to interact with your secured service to update or add credentials.

**Topics**

- Permissions Required to Automatically Rotate Secrets
- Rotating Secrets for Supported Amazon RDS Databases
- Rotating AWS Secrets Manager Secrets for Other Databases or Services
- Understanding and Customizing Your Lambda Rotation Function
- Deleting Lambda Rotation Functions That You No Longer Need

52

# Permissions Required to Automatically Rotate Secrets

When you use the AWS Secrets Manager console to configure rotation for a secret for one of the fully supported databases, the console configures just about everything for you. So you shouldn't have to manually configure the permissions described in this section. But if you create your own rotation function or choose to do anything manually for other reasons, you might have to also manually configure the permissions for that part of the rotation.

## Permissions Associated with the Lambda Rotation Function

AWS Secrets Manager uses a Lambda function to implement the code that actually rotates the credentials in a secret.

The Lambda function is invoked by the Secrets Manager service itself. The service does this by invoking an IAM role that's attached to the Lambda function. There are two pieces to this:

- **The *trust policy* that specifies who can assume the role.** You must configure this policy to allow Secrets Manager to assume the role, as identified by its service principal: `secretsmanager.amazonaws.com`. This policy is viewable in the Lambda console on the function details page by clicking the key icon in the **Designer** section. It then appears in the **Function policy** section. This policy should look similar to the following example:

```
1 {
2   "Version": "2012-10-17",
3   "Id": "default",
4   "Statement": [
5     {
6       "Sid": "EXAMPLE1-90ab-cdef-fedc-ba987EXAMPLE",
7       "Effect": "Allow",
8       "Principal": {
9         "Service": "secretsmanager.amazonaws.com"
10      },
11      "Action": "lambda:InvokeFunction",
12      "Resource": "<arn of the Lambda function that this trust policy is attached to - must
            match exactly>"
13    }
14  ]
15 }
```

For security reasons, the trust policy created by Secrets Manager includes a `Resource` element that includes the Amazon Resource Name (ARN) of the Lambda function. That results in anyone who assumes the role being able to invoke *only* the Lambda function that's associated with the role.

- **The *permissions policy* for the role that specifies what the assumer of the role can do.** You must configure this policy to specify the permissions that Secrets Manager can use when it assumes the role by invoking the function. There are two different policies, depending on the rotation strategy you want to implement.

  - **Single user rotation**: The following example is suitable for a function that rotates a secret by signing in with the credentials that are stored in that secret, and changing its own password.

```
1 {
2     "Statement": [
3         {
4             "Effect": "Allow",
5             "Action": [
```

53

```
6              "secretsmanager:DescribeSecret",
7              "secretsmanager:GetSecretValue",
8              "secretsmanager:PutSecretValue",
9              "secretsmanager:UpdateSecretVersionStage"
10          ],
11          "Resource": "*",
12          "Condition": {
13              "StringEquals": {
14                  "secretsmanager:resource/AllowRotationLambdaArn": "<lambda_arn>"
15              }
16          }
17      },
18      {
19          "Effect": "Allow",
20          "Action": [
21              "secretsmanager:GetRandomPassword"
22          ],
23          "Resource": "*"
24      },
25      {
26          "Action": [
27              "ec2:CreateNetworkInterface",
28              "ec2:DeleteNetworkInterface",
29              "ec2:DescribeNetworkInterfaces",
30              "ec2:DetachNetworkInterface"
31          ],
32          "Resource": "*",
33          "Effect": "Allow"
34      }
35  ]
36 }
```

The first statement in the single-user example grants permission to the function to run Secrets Manager operations. However, the `Condition` element restricts this to only secrets that are configured with this Lambda function's ARN as the secret's rotation Lambda function.

The second statement allows one additional Secrets Manager operation that doesn't require the condition.

The third statement enables Lambda to set up the required configuration when you specify that your database or service is running in a VPC. For more information, see Configuring a Lambda Function to Access Resources in an Amazon VPC in the *AWS Lambda Developer Guide*.

- **Master user rotation**: The following example is suitable for a function that rotates a secret by signing in using a separate "master" secret that contains credentials with elevated permissions. This is typically required when you use one of the rotation strategies that alternate between two users.

```
1 {
2      "Statement": [
3          {
4              "Effect": "Allow",
5              "Action": [
6                  "secretsmanager:DescribeSecret",
7                  "secretsmanager:GetSecretValue",
8                  "secretsmanager:PutSecretValue",
9                  "secretsmanager:UpdateSecretVersionStage"
10              ],
```

```
11        "Resource": "*",
12        "Condition": {
13            "StringEquals": {
14                "secretsmanager:resource/AllowRotationLambdaArn": "<lambda_arn>"
15            }
16        }
17    },
18    {
19        "Effect": "Allow",
20        "Action": [
21            "secretsmanager:GetRandomPassword"
22        ],
23        "Resource": "*"
24    },
25    {
26        "Action": [
27            "ec2:CreateNetworkInterface",
28            "ec2:DeleteNetworkInterface",
29            "ec2:DescribeNetworkInterfaces",
30            "ec2:DetachNetworkInterface"
31        ],
32        "Resource": "*",
33        "Effect": "Allow"
34    },
35    {
36        "Effect": "Allow",
37        "Action": [
38            "secretsmanager:GetSecretValue"
39        ],
40        "Resource": "<master_arn>"
41    }
42    ]
43 }
```

In addition to the same three statements as the previous single-user policy, this policy adds a fourth statement. The fourth statement enables the function to retrieve the credentials in the master secret. The credentials in the master secret are used to sign in to the secured database to update the credentials in the secret that's being rotated.

# Rotating Secrets for Supported Amazon RDS Databases

You can configure AWS Secrets Manager to automatically rotate the secret for an Amazon RDS database. Secrets Manager uses a Lambda function that Secrets Manager provides.

**Supported Amazon RDS Databases**

For the purposes of the Amazon RDS options in Secrets Manager, a "supported" database means that when you enable rotation, Secrets Manager provides a complete, ready-to-run Lambda rotation function that's designed for that database. For any other type of Amazon RDS database, you can still rotate your secret. However, you must use the workflow for **Other database**. For those instructions, see Rotating AWS Secrets Manager Secrets for Other Databases or Services.

The following list shows the Amazon RDS databases for which Secrets Manager provides and configures a complete, ready-to-use rotation function for you, without any additional steps.

- Amazon Aurora on Amazon RDS
- MySQL running on Amazon RDS
- PostgreSQL running on Amazon RDS

When you enable rotation for a secret with **Credentials for RDS database** as the secret type, Secrets Manager automatically creates and configures a Lambda rotation function for you, and then equips your secret with the Amazon Resource Name (ARN) of the function. Secrets Manager creates the IAM role that's associated with the function and configures it with all of the required permissions.

If your Amazon RDS database is running in a VPC provided by Amazon VPC, Secrets Manager also configures the Lambda function to communicate with that VPC. The only requirement of the VPC is that it must have an NAT gateway to enable the Lambda rotation function to query the Secrets Manager service endpoint on the internet.

Otherwise, you typically only need to provide a few details that determine which template is used to construct the Lambda function:

- **Specify the secret that has credentials with permissions to rotate the secret**: Sometimes the user can change their own password. Other times, the user has very restricted permissions and can't change their own password. Instead, you must use the credentials for a different administrator or "super" user to change the user's credentials.

  You must specify which secret the rotation function can use to rotate the credentials on the secured database:

  - **Use this secret**: Choose this option if the credentials in the current secret have permissions in the database to change its own password. Choosing this option causes Secrets Manager to implement a Lambda function with a rotation strategy that changes the password for a single user with each rotation. For more information about this rotation strategy, see Rotating AWS Secrets Manager Secrets for One User with a Single Password. **Considerations**
    This option is the "lower availability" option. This is because sign-in failures can occur between the moment when the old password is removed by the rotation and the moment when the updated password is made accessible as the new version of the secret. This time window is typically very short—on the order of a second or less. If you choose this option, make sure that your client apps implement an appropriate "backoff and retry with jitter" strategy in their code. The apps should generate an error only if sign-in fails several times over a longer period of time.
  - **Use a secret that I have previously stored in AWS Secrets Manager**: Choose this option if the credentials in the current secret have more restrictive permissions and can't be used to update the credentials on the secured service. Or choose this if you require high availability for the secret. To choose this option, create a separate "master" secret with credentials that have permission to create and update credentials on the secured service. Then choose that master secret from the list. Choosing this option causes Secrets Manager to implement a Lambda function. This Lambda function has a rotation strategy that clones the initial user that's found in the secret. Then it alternates between the

two users with each rotation, and updates the password for the user that's becoming active. For more information about this rotation strategy, see Rotating AWS Secrets Manager Secrets by Alternating Between Two Existing Users. **Considerations**

This is the "high availability" option because the old version of the secret continues to operate and handle service requests while the new version is prepared and tested. The old version isn't deprecated until after the clients switch to the new version. There's no downtime while changing between versions. This option requires the Lambda function to clone the permissions of the original user and apply them to the new user. The function then alternates between the two users with each rotation.

If you ever need to change the permissions granted to the users, ensure that you change permissions for both users.

- **You can customize the function**: You can tailor the Lambda rotation function that's provided by Secrets Manager to meet your organization's requirements. For example, you could extend the **testSecret** phase of the function to test the new version with application-specific checks to ensure that the new secret works as expected. For instructions, see Customizing the Lambda Rotation Function Provided by Secrets Manager.

**Topics**

- Enabling Rotation for an Amazon RDS Database Secret
- Customizing the Lambda Rotation Function Provided by Secrets Manager

# Enabling Rotation for an Amazon RDS Database Secret

You can enable rotation for a secret that has credentials for a supported Amazon RDS database by using the AWS Secrets Manager console, the AWS CLI, or one of the AWS SDKs.

**Warning**

Enabling rotation causes the secret to rotate once immediately when you save the secret. Before you enable rotation, ensure that all of your applications that use this secret's credentials are updated to retrieve the secret from Secrets Manager. The original credentials might not be usable after the initial rotation. Any applications that you fail to update break as soon as the old credentials are no longer valid.

**Prerequisites: Network Requirements to Enable Rotation**

To successfully enable rotation, you must have your network environment configured correctly.

- **The Lambda function must be able to communicate with the database.** If your RDS database instance is running in a VPC, we recommend that you configure your Lambda function to run in the same VPC. This enables direct connectivity between the rotation function and your service. To configure this, on the Lambda function's details page, scroll down to the **Network** section and choose the **VPC** from the drop-down list to match the one your instance is running in. You must also make sure that the EC2 security groups attached to your instance enable communication between the instance and Lambda.
- **The Lambda function must be able to communicate with the Secrets Manager service endpoint.** Each of the available endpoints for Secrets Manager is on the public Internet, so your Lambda must be able to access the Internet. If your database instance and your Lambda rotation function reside in a VPC, you must provide a way for resources in the VPC to connect to the Internet. You can do this by adding a NAT Gateway or Internet Gateway to your VPC.

**To enable and configure rotation for a supported Amazon RDS database secret**

Follow the steps under one of the following tabs:

---

[ **Using the AWS Management Console** ]

**Minimum permissions**

To enable and configure rotation in the console, you must have the permissions that are provided by the following managed policies:

`SecretsManagerReadWrite` – Provides all of the Secrets Manager, Lambda, and AWS CloudFormation permissions. `IAMFullAccess` – Provides the IAM permissions that are required to create a role and attach a permission policy to it.

1. Sign in to the AWS Secrets Manager console at https://console.aws.amazon.com/secretsmanager/.

2. Choose the name of the secret that you want to enable rotation for.

3. In the **Configure automatic rotation** section, choose **Enable automatic rotation**. This enables the other controls in this section.

4. For **Select rotation interval**, choose one of the predefined values—or choose **Custom**, and then type the number of days you want between rotations. If you're rotating your secret to meet compliance requirements, then we recommend that you set this value to at least 1 day less than the compliance-mandated interval.
   **Note**
   If you use the Lambda function that's provided by Secrets Manager to alternate between two users (the console uses this template if you choose the second "master secret" option in the next step), then you should set your rotation period to one-half of your compliance-specified minimum interval. This is because the old credentials are still available (if not actively used) for one additional rotation cycle. The old credentials are fully invalidated only after the user is updated with a new password after the second rotation.
   If you modify the rotation function to immediately invalidate the old credentials after the new secret becomes active, then you can extend the rotation interval to your full compliance-mandated minimum.

Leaving the old credentials active for one additional cycle with the `AWSPREVIOUS` staging label provides a "last known good" set of credentials that you can use for fast recovery. If something happens that breaks the current credentials, you can simply move the `AWSCURRENT` staging label to the version that has the `AWSPREVIOUS` label. Then your customers should be able to access the resource again. For more information, see Rotating AWS Secrets Manager Secrets by Alternating Between Two Existing Users.

5. Specify the secret with credentials that the rotation function can use to update the credentials on the protected database.

   - **Use this secret**: Choose this option if the credentials in this secret have permission in the database to change their own password. Choosing this option causes Secrets Manager to implement a Lambda function that rotates secrets with a single user that gets its password changed with each rotation. **Note**
   This option is the "lower availability" option. This is because sign-in failures can occur between the moment when the old password is removed by the rotation and the moment when the updated password is made accessible as a new version of the secret. This time window should be very short, on the order of a few seconds or less, but it can happen.
   If you choose the **Use this secret** option, ensure that your client apps that sign in with the secret use an appropriate "backoff and retry with jitter" strategy in code. A real failure should be reported only if signing in fails several times over a longer period of time.

   - **Use a secret that I have previously stored in AWS Secrets Manager**: Choose this option if the credentials in the current secret don't have permissions to update the credentials, or you require high availability for the secret. To choose this option, you must create a separate "master" secret with credentials that have permissions to update the current secret's credentials. Then choose the master secret from the list. Choosing this option causes Secrets Manager to implement a Lambda function that rotates secrets by creating a new user and password with each rotation, and deprecating the old one. **Note**
   This is the "high availability" option because the old version of the secret continues to operate and handle service requests while the new version is prepared and tested. The old version is not deleted until after the clients switch to the new version. There's no downtime while changing between versions. This option requires the Lambda function to clone the permissions of the original user and apply them to the new user in each rotation.

6. Choose **Save** to store your changes and to trigger the initial rotation of the secret.

7. If you chose to rotate your secret with a separate master secret, then you must manually grant your Lambda rotation function permission to access the master secret. Follow these instructions:

   1. When rotation configuration completes, the following message appears at the top of the page:

      *Your secret has been successfully stored and secret rotation is enabled. To finish configuring rotation, you need to provide the *role* permissions to access the value of the secret ***.

      You must manually modify the policy for the role to grant the rotation function GetSecretValue access to the master secret. Secrets Manager can't do this for you for security reasons. Rotation of the secret fails until you complete the following steps because it can't access the master secret.

   2. Copy the Amazon Resource Name (ARN) from the message to your clipboard.

   3. Choose the link on the word "role" in the message. This opens the IAM console to the role details page for the role attached to the Lambda rotation function that Secrets Manager created for you.

   4. On the **Permissions** tab, choose **Add inline policy**, and then set the following values:

      - For **Service**, choose **Secrets Manager**.
      - For **Actions**, choose **GetSecretValue**.
      - For **Resources**, choose **Add ARN** next to the **secret** resource type entry.
      - In the **Add ARN(s)** dialog box, paste the ARN of the master secret that you copied previously.

5. Choose **Review policy**, and then choose **Create policy**. **Note**
As an alternative to using the Visual Editor as described in the previous steps, you can paste the following statement into an existing or new policy:

```
1 {
2     "Effect": "Allow",
3     "Action": "secretsmanager:GetSecretValue",
4     "Resource": "<ARN of the master secret>"
5 }
```

6. Return to the AWS Secrets Manager console.

If there's not already an ARN for a Lambda function that's assigned to the secret, Secrets Manager creates the function, assigns all required permissions, and configures it to work with your database. Secrets Manager counts down the number of days specified in the rotation interval. When it reaches zero, Secrets Manager rotates the secret again and resets the interval for the next cycle. This continues until you disable rotation.

---

## [ Using the AWS CLI or SDK Operations ]

### Minimum permissions

To enable and configure rotation in the console, you must have the permissions that are provided by the following managed policies:
`SecretsManagerReadWrite` – Provides all of the Secrets Manager, Lambda, and AWS CloudFormation permissions. `IAMFullAccess` – Provides the IAM permissions that are required to create a role and attach a permission policy to it.

You can use the following Secrets Manager commands to configure rotation for an existing secret for a supported Amazon RDS database:

- **API/SDK:** RotateSecret
- **AWS CLI:** RotateSecret

You also need to use commands from AWS CloudFormation and AWS Lambda. For more information about the commands that follow, see the documentation for those services.

### To create a Lambda rotation function by using an AWS Serverless Application Repository template

The following is an example AWS CLI session that performs the equivalent of the console-based rotation configuration that's described in the **Using the AWS Management Console** tab. You create the function by using an AWS CloudFormation change set. Then you configure the resulting function with the required permissions. Finally, you configure the secret with the ARN of the completed function, and rotate once to test it.

The following example uses the generic template, so it uses the last ARN that was shown earlier.

If your database or service resides in a VPC provided by Amazon VPC, then you must include the fourth command below that configures the function to communicate with that VPC. If no VPC is involved, then you can skip that command.

The first command sets up an AWS CloudFormation change set based on the template provided by Secrets Manager.

You use the `--application-id` parameter to specify which template to use. The value is the ARN of the template. For the list of templates provided by AWS and their ARNs, see AWS Templates You Can Use to Create Lambda Rotation Functions .

The templates also require additional parameters that are provided with `--parameter-overrides`, as shown in the example that follows. This parameter is required to pass two pieces of information as Name and Value pairs to the template that affect how the rotation function is created:

- **endpoint** – The URL of the service endpoint that you want the rotation function to query. Typically, this is `https://secretsmanager.region.amazonaws.com`.
- **functionname** – The name of the completed Lambda rotation function that's created by this process.

```
1 $ aws serverlessrepo create-cloud-formation-change-set \
2         --application-id arn:aws:serverlessrepo:us-east-1:297356227824:applications/
          SecretsManagerRotationTemplate \
3         --parameter-overrides '[{"Name":"endpoint","Value":"https://secretsmanager.region.
          amazonaws.com"},{"Name":"functionName","Value":"MyLambdaRotationFunction"}]' \
4         --stack-name MyLambdaCreationStack
5 {
6     "ApplicationId": "arn:aws:serverlessrepo:us-west-2:297356227824:applications/
        SecretsManagerRDSMySQLRotationSingleUser",
7     "ChangeSetId": "arn:aws:cloudformation:us-west-2:123456789012:changeSet/EXAMPLE1-90ab-cdef-
        fedc-ba987EXAMPLE/EXAMPLE2-90ab-cdef-fedc-ba987EXAMPLE",
8     "StackId": "arn:aws:cloudformation:us-west-2:123456789012:stack/aws-serverless-repository-
        MyLambdaCreationStack/EXAMPLE3-90ab-cdef-fedc-ba987EXAMPLE"
9 }
```

The next command runs the change set that you just created. The change-set-name parameter comes from the `ChangeSetId` output of the previous command. This command produces no output.

```
1 $ aws cloudformation execute-change-set --change-set-name arn:aws:cloudformation:us-west
  -2:123456789012:changeSet/EXAMPLE1-90ab-cdef-fedc-ba987EXAMPLE/EXAMPLE2-90ab-cdef-fedc-
  ba987EXAMPLE
```

The following command grants the Secrets Manager service permission to call the function on your behalf. The output shows the permission added to the role's trust policy.

```
1 $ aws lambda add-permission \
2         --function-name MyLambdaRotationFunction \
3         --principal secretsmanager.amazonaws.com \
4         --action lambda:InvokeFunction \
5         --statement-id SecretsManagerAccess
6 {
7     "Statement": "{\"Sid\":\"SecretsManagerAccess\",\"Effect\":\"Allow\",\"Principal\":{\"
        Service\":\"secretsmanager.amazonaws.com\"},\"Action\":\"lambda:InvokeFunction\",\"
        Resource\":\"arn:aws:lambda:us-west-2:123456789012:function:MyLambdaRotationFunction\"}"
8 }
```

The following command is required only if your database is running in a VPC. If it isn't, skip this command. Look up the VPC information for your Amazon RDS instance by using either the Amazon RDS console, or by using the `aws rds describe-instances` CLI command. Then put that information in the following command and run it.

```
1 $ aws lambda update-function-configuration \
2         --function-name arn:aws:lambda:us-west-2:123456789012:function:
          MyLambdaRotationFunction \
3         --vpc-config SubnetIds=<COMMA SEPARATED LIST OF VPC SUBNET IDS>,SecurityGroupIds=<
          COMMA SEPARATED LIST OF SECURITY GROUP IDs>
```

If you created a function using a template that requires a master secret, then you must also add the following statement to the function's role policy. For complete instructions, see Granting a Rotation Function Permission to Access a Separate Master Secret.

```
1         {
2             "Action": "secretsmanager:GetSecretValue",
```

```
3            "Resource": "arn:aws:secretsmanager:region:123456789012:secret:
                MyDatabaseMasterSecret",
4            "Effect": "Allow"
5        },
```

Finally, you can apply the rotation configuration to your secret and perform the initial rotation.

```
1 $ aws secretsmanager rotate-secret \
2          --secret-id production/MyAwesomeAppSecret \
3          --rotation-lambda-arn arn:aws:lambda:us-west-2:123456789012:function:aws-serverless-
                repository-SecretsManagerRDSMySQLRo-10WGBDAXQ6ZEH \
4          --rotation-rules AutomaticallyAfterDays=7
```

We recommend that even if you want to create your own Lambda rotation function for a supported Amazon RDS database, you should follow the preceding steps that use the SecretsManagerRotationTemplate AWS CloudFormation template. This is because it lets Secrets Manager set up most of the permissions and configuration settings for you.

_____

# Customizing the Lambda Rotation Function Provided by Secrets Manager

You can customize the Lambda rotation function to meet your organization's unique requirements. Such requirements might include:

- Add additional tests on the new version of the secret. You want to ensure that the permissions associated with the new credentials are correct.
- You want to use a different strategy for rotating your secrets than the one used by the Lambda function provided by Secrets Manager.

To customize the function, you must first discover which function Secrets Manager created for you. You can't see the ARN of the function in the console, but you can retrieve it by using the AWS CLI or equivalent AWS SDK operations.

```
1 $ aws secretsmanager describe-secret --secret-id MyDatabaseSecret
```

Look for the `RotationLambdaARN` value in the response.

**To edit your Lambda rotation function**
Follow the steps under one of the following tabs:

---

**[ Using the console ]**

1. Determine the name of the Lambda rotation function for your secret:

    1. On the list of secrets, choose the name of the secret whose rotation you want to modify.

    2. In the **Rotation configuration** section, examine the rotation ARN. The part of the ARN that follows `:function:` is the name.

2. Open the AWS Lambda console at https://console.aws.amazon.com/lambda/.

3. Choose the name of the Lambda rotation function that you want to modify.

4. Make the required changes to the function.

---

**[ Using the AWS CLI or AWS SDK operations ]**

1. Determine the name of the Lambda rotation function for your secret. To do this, run the following command and examine the part of the `RotationLambdaARN` that follows `:function:`.

```
1 $ describe-secret --secret-id MySecret
2 {
3     "ARN": "arn:aws:secretsmanager:us-west-2:123456789012:secret:MySecret-abc123",
4     "Name": "MySecret",
5     "RotationLambdaARN": "arn:aws:lambda:us-west-2:123456789012:function:
        name_of_rotation_lambda_function",
6     "LastChangedDate": 1519940941.014,
7     "SecretVersionsToStages": {
8         "5eae5e4a-a683-469e-96e7-af9a8180fba5": [
9             "AWSCURRENT"
10         ]
11     }
12 }
```

2. Examine the `RotationLambdaARN` response value. That is the ARN of your Lambda rotation function and the last portion is the name of your function.

3. Sign in to the AWS Management Console and open the AWS Lambda console at https://console.aws.amazon.com/lambda/.

4. Choose the name of the Lambda function that you identified to see the function details.

5. In the **Function code** section, you can edit the source code of the function. For more information about coding a Lambda function specifically for Secrets Manager, see Overview of the Lambda Rotation Function. For the http://docs.aws.amazon.com/lambda/latest/dg/. All of the provided Lambda functions are written for the Python 2.7 environment.

---

For more information about Lambda function options and coding techniques, see the AWS Lambda Developer Guide.

For more information about coding your own Secrets Manager rotation function, see Understanding and Customizing Your Lambda Rotation Function.

# Rotating AWS Secrets Manager Secrets for Other Databases or Services

If you create a secret for anything other than one of the supported Amazon RDS databases, then AWS Secrets Manager doesn't create the Lambda rotation function for you. You must create and configure it, and then provide the Amazon Resource Name (ARN) of the completed function to the secret. You do this by using the Secrets Manager console, the AWS CLI, or one of the AWS SDKs.

The procedure in this topic describes how to create the Lambda function by using an AWS CloudFormation change set that you create and run. You then attach some permissions. At that point, you can edit the code to make the rotation function work the way you want it to. Finally, you associate the completed function with your secret so that Secrets Manager calls the function every time rotation is triggered.

You can specify the "generic" template that you must fully implement. Or you can choose one of the templates that completely implement a rotation strategy for a certain database or service, and use that as a starting point to customize the function to meet your needs.

### Minimum permissions

To run the commands that enable and configure rotation, you must have the following permissions:
`serverlessrepo:CreateCloudFormationChangeSet` – To create the AWS CloudFormation change set that configures and creates the Lambda rotation function. `cloudformation:ExecuteChangeSet` – To run the AWS CloudFormation change set that creates and configures the Lambda rotation function. `lambda:AddPermission` – To add the required permissions to the Lambda rotation function after it's created. `lambda:InvokeFunction` – To attach the rotation function to the secret. `lambda:UpdateFunctionConfiguration` – To allow the console to update the VPC configuration of the Lambda function so it can communicate with a database or service that resides in a VPC. `secretsmanager:RotateSecret` – To configure and trigger the initial rotation. You can grant all of these permissions to an IAM user or role by attaching the SecretsManagerReadWrite AWS managed policy.

The commands that follow apply the generic `SecretsManagerRotationTemplate` to your Lambda function. This template comes from the AWS Serverless Application Repository, and is used by AWS CloudFormation to automate most of the steps for you. For the complete set of templates and the ARN that you must specify, see AWS Templates You Can Use to Create Lambda Rotation Functions .

The ARN of the generic template is as follows. It must be entered exactly as shown:

```
1 arn:aws:serverlessrepo:us-east-1:297356227824:applications/SecretsManagerRotationTemplate
```

If the database or service that your credentials are for resides in a VPC provided by Amazon VPC, then you must include the command in step 5. (This command configures the function to communicate with that VPC.) If no VPC is involved, then you can skip that command.

**To create a Lambda rotation function as a generic template to customize**

1. The first command sets up an AWS CloudFormation change set based on the template that's provided by Secrets Manager. You provide two parameters to the template: the Secrets Manager endpoint URL and the name that you want to give to the Lambda rotation function that the template produces.

```
1 $ aws serverlessrepo create-cloud-formation-change-set \
2       --application-id arn:aws:serverlessrepo:us-east-1:297356227824:applications/
          SecretsManagerRotationTemplate \
3       --stack-name MyLambdaCreationStack \
4       --parameter-overrides '[{"Name":"endpoint","Value":"https://secretsmanager.region
          .amazonaws.com"},{"Name":"functionName","Value":"
          MySecretsManagerRotationFuncion"}]'
5 {
6     "ApplicationId": "arn:aws:serverlessrepo:us-east-1:297356227824:applications/
          SecretsManagerRDSMySQLRotationSingleUser",
```

```
7        "ChangeSetId": "arn:aws:cloudformation:region:123456789012:changeSet/EXAMPLE1-90ab-cdef
           -fedc-ba987EXAMPLE/EXAMPLE2-90ab-cdef-fedc-ba987EXAMPLE",
8        "StackId": "arn:aws:cloudformation:region:123456789012:stack/aws-serverless-repository-
           MyLambdaCreationStack/EXAMPLE3-90ab-cdef-fedc-ba987EXAMPLE"
9  }
```

2. The next command runs the change set that you just created. The change-set-name parameter comes from the `ChangeSetId` output of the previous command. This command produces no output:

```
1  $ aws cloudformation execute-change-set --change-set-name arn:aws:cloudformation:region
     :123456789012:changeSet/EXAMPLE1-90ab-cdef-fedc-ba987EXAMPLE/EXAMPLE2-90ab-cdef-fedc-
     ba987EXAMPLE
```

3. Next, you must find the name of the Lambda function that the previous command just created for you. The function name begins with `aws-serverless-repository-` followed by the first 24 characters of the template's name followed by a dash and a random string of characters.

```
1  $ aws lambda list-functions
2  {
3      ...
4      "FunctionName": "MySecretsManagerRotationFuncion",
5      "FunctionArn": "arn:aws:lambda:us-west-2:123456789012:function:
           MySecretsManagerRotationFuncion",
6      ...
7  }
```

4. The following command grants Secrets Manager permission to call the function on your behalf.

```
1  $ aws lambda add-permission \
2            --function-name MySecretsManagerRotationFunction \
3            --principal secretsmanager.amazonaws.com \
4            --action lambda:InvokeFunction \
5            --statement-id SecretsManagerAccess
6  {
7      "Statement": "{\"Sid\":\"SecretsManagerAccess\",\"Effect\":\"Allow\",\"Principal\":{\"
           Service\":\"secretsmanager.amazonaws.com\"},\"Action\":\"lambda:InvokeFunction\",\"
           Resource\":\"arn:aws:lambda:us-west-2:123456789012:function:aws-serverless-
           repository-SecretsManagerRDSMySQLRo-10WGBDAXQ6ZEH\"}"
8  }
```

5. The following command is required only if your database is running in a VPC. If it isn't, skip this command. Look up the VPC information for your Amazon RDS database instance by using either the Amazon RDS console, or by using the `aws rds describe-instances` CLI command. Then put that information in the following command and run it.

```
1  $ aws lambda update-function-configuration \
2            --function-name arn:aws:lambda:us-west-2:123456789012:function:
             MySecretsManagerRotationFuncion \
3            --vpc-config SubnetIds=<COMMA SEPARATED LIST OF VPC SUBNET IDS>,SecurityGroupIds
             =<COMMA SEPARATED LIST OF SECURITY GROUP IDs> \
```

6. At this point, your Lambda rotation function is ready for you to enter the code.

Open the AWS Lambda console at https://console.aws.amazon.com/lambda/.

7. Customize the code to implement your chosen rotation scenario. For details, see Understanding and Customizing Your Lambda Rotation Function.

8. Finally, you can apply the rotation configuration to your secret and perform the initial rotation. Specify the number of days between successive rotations with the `--rotation-rules` parameter, and set `AutomaticallyAfterDays` to the number of days you want.

```
1 $ aws secretsmanager rotate-secret \
2           --secret-id production/MyAwesomeAppSecret \
3           --rotation-lambda-arn arn:aws:lambda:us-west-2:123456789012:function:
              MySecretsManagerRotationFuncion \
4           --rotation-rules AutomaticallyAfterDays=7
```

The secret rotates once immediately, and then begins to rotate as frequently as you specified.

# Enabling Rotation for a Secret for Another Database or Service

To configure rotation of a secret for a database other than the supported RDS databases or some other service, you must manually perform a few extra steps. Primarily, you must create and provide the code for the Lambda rotation function.

**Warning**

Configuring rotation causes the secret to rotate once as soon as you store the secret. Before you do this, you must make sure that all of your applications that use the credentials stored in the secret are updated to retrieve the secret from AWS Secrets Manager. The old credentials might not be usable after the initial rotation. Any applications that you fail to update break as soon as the old credentials are no longer valid.

You must have already created your Lambda rotation function. If you haven't yet created the function, then perform the steps in Rotating AWS Secrets Manager Secrets for Other Databases or Services. Return to this procedure when the function is created and ready to associate with your secret.

**Prerequisites: Network Requirements to Enable Rotation**

To successfully enable rotation, you must have your network environment configured correctly.

- **The Lambda function must be able to communicate with your database or service.** If your database or service is running on an Amazon EC2 instance in a VPC, then we recommend that you configure your Lambda function to run in the same VPC. This enables direct connectivity between the rotation function and your service. To configure this, on the Lambda function's details page, scroll down to the **Network** section and choose the **VPC** from the drop-down list to match the one the instance with your service is running in. You must also make sure that the EC2 security groups attached to your instance enable communication between the instance and Lambda.
- **The Lambda function must be able to communicate with the Secrets Manager service endpoint.** Each of the available endpoints for Secrets Manager is on the public Internet, so your Lambda must be able to access the Internet. If your service and Lambda rotation function reside in a VPC, you must provide a way for resources in the VPC to connect to the Internet. You can do this by adding a NAT Gateway or Internet Gateway to your VPC.

**To enable and configure rotation for a secret for another database or service**

Follow the steps under one of the following tabs:

---

[ **Using the AWS Management Console** ]

**Minimum permissions**

To enable and configure rotation in the console, you must have these permissions:
`secretsmanager:ListSecrets` – To see the list of secrets in the console. `secretsmanager:DescribeSecrets` – To access the details page for your chosen secret. `secretsmanager:RotateSecret` – To configure or trigger rotation.

1. Sign in to the Secrets Manager console at https://console.aws.amazon.com/secretsmanager/.

2. Choose the name of the secret that you want to enable rotation for.

3. In the **Configure automatic rotation** section, choose **Enable automatic rotation**. This enables the other controls in this section.

4. For **Select rotation interval**, choose one of the predefined values—or choose **Custom**, and then type the number of days you want between rotations.

5. For **Choose an AWS Lambda function**, choose your rotation function from the drop-down list. If you haven't yet created the function, perform the steps in Rotating AWS Secrets Manager Secrets for Other Databases or Services. Return and perform this step when the function is created and ready to associate with your secret.

## [ Using the AWS CLI or AWS SDKs ]

### Minimum permissions

To create a Lambda function by using the console, you must have these permissions:
`lambda:CreateFunction` – To create the function in AWS Lambda. `lambda:InvokeFunction` – To attach the rotation function to the secret. `secretsmanager:DescribeSecrets` – To access the secret details page. `secretsmanager:RotateSecret` – To attach the rotation function to the secret or to trigger rotation.

You can use the following commands to enable and configure rotation in Secrets Manager:

- **API/SDK:** http://docs.aws.amazon.com/secretsmanager/latest/apireference/API_RotateSecret.html
- **AWS CLI:** http://docs.aws.amazon.com/cli/latest/reference/secretsmanager/rotate-secret.html

### Example

The following is an example CLI command that performs the equivalent of the console-based secret creation in the **Using the AWS Management Console** tab. It sets the rotation interval to 30 days, and specifies the Amazon Resource Name (ARN) of a second secret that has permissions to change this secret's credentials on the database.

```
1 $ aws secretsmanager rotate-secret --secret-id production/MyAwesomeAppSecret --automatically-
    rotate-after-days 30 --rotation-lambda-arn arn:aws:secretsmanager:region:accountid:secret:
    production/MasterSecret-AbCdEf
2 {
3     "ARN": "arn:aws:secretsmanager:region:accountid:secret:production/MyAwesomeAppSecret-AbCdEf
        ",
4     "Name": "production/MyAwesomeAppSecret",
5     "VersionId": "EXAMPLE1-90ab-cdef-fedc-ba987EXAMPLE"
6 }
```

The `ClientRequestToken` parameter isn't required because we're using the AWS CLI, which automatically generates and supplies one for us. The output includes the secret version ID of the new version that's created during the initial rotation. After rotation is completed, this new version has the staging label `AWSCURRENT` attached, and the previous version has the staging label `AWSPREVIOUS`.

# Understanding and Customizing Your Lambda Rotation Function

For details about how a Lambda rotation function works, see Overview of the Lambda Rotation Function.

If you choose one of the supported databases for your secret type, AWS Secrets Manager creates and configures the Lambda rotation function for you. You can enable rotation for those databases by following the steps in Enabling Rotation for an Amazon RDS Database Secret. However, if you want to create a custom Lambda rotation function for another service, then you must follow the steps in Enabling Rotation for a Secret for Another Database or Service.

This section describes in detail how the Lambda function operates and how it needs to be configured to successfully rotate your secrets.

**Important**
The Lambda function and the Secrets Manager secret that invokes it must be in the same AWS Region. If they're in different regions, you get a "Lambda does not exist" error message when you try to add the Amazon Resource Name (ARN) of the function to the secret's metadata.

The following are the primary scenarios to consider when you're creating your own Lambda function for rotation. The scenario that applies is determined by the features supported by the authentication system that protects the secured resource, and by your security concerns.

- **You can change only the password for a single user.** This is a common scenario for services that are owned by someone other than the user who accesses the service. The owner of the service lets the customer create *one* user account, often with something like the user's email address as the user name itself, or at least as a uniqueness key. In this scenario, the service typically allows the user to change the password as often as is required. But, it doesn't allow the user to create additional users, and often doesn't even allow the user name to change.

  Users typically have the ability to change their own password, and don't require a separate user with administrator permissions to do the password change. However, because you're changing the password for the single, active user, clients that access the service with this user might temporarily fail to sign in while the password change is in progress.

  The potential for downtime exists between when the password is changed and when the clients all get notified to use the newer version of the password. This should typically be only on the order of a few seconds, and you must allow for it in your application code that uses the secret. Be sure to enable retries with some delay in between to be tolerant of this short-term outage during a rotation.

- **You can create two users that you can alternate between.** In this scenario, you can create one user that the rotation process clones to make two users that have equal access to the secured resource. The rotation process alternates between the two users. It changes the password, and tests the "inactive" one while your users continue to access the database or service by using the credentials in the "active" secret.

  While your clients are all accessing the secured resource with one user name (by querying for the version that has the default staging label `AWSCURRENT` attached), the rotation function changes the password on the currently inactive second user. The rotation function stores that updated password in a new version of the secret that has the staging label `AWSCURRENT`. After testing, you move the staging label `AWSCURRENT` to the new version that points to the alternate user and its new password. All of the clients immediately begin accessing the secured resource with the alternate user and its updated password.

  When it's time for the next rotation, you change the password on the original user account that's now idle. This creates another new version of the secret and repeats the cycle.

  This scenario requires a second secret that points to an administrator or super user that has permissions to change the password on both users.

- **You can create new credentials for a single user.** Some systems enable you to create a single user with multiple sets of access credentials. Each access credential is a complete set of credentials and operates independently of the other. You can delete and recreate the first access credential while the second access credential is in use. Then you can switch all of your clients to use the new first access credential. The next time you rotate, you delete and recreate the second access credential while customers to continue to use the second.

For additional details and instructions on how to configure each scenario, see the following topics:

- Overview of the Lambda Rotation Function
- Rotating AWS Secrets Manager Secrets for One User with a Single Password
- Rotating AWS Secrets Manager Secrets by Alternating Between Two Existing Users
- Rotating AWS Secrets Manager Secrets For One User that Supports Multiple Credentials

# Overview of the Lambda Rotation Function

AWS Secrets Manager uses an AWS Lambda function to perform the actual rotation of a secret. If your secret is for one of the supported Amazon RDS databases, then Secrets Manager provides the Lambda function for you. And it automatically customizes the function to meet the requirements of the database that you specify. If your secret is for some other service, then you must provide the code for the Lambda function yourself.

When rotation is triggered, either by a configured rotation schedule or by you triggering it manually, Secrets Manager calls the Lambda function several times, each time with different parameters. The Lambda function is expected to perform several tasks throughout the process of rotating a secret. The task to be performed for each request is specified by the `type` parameter in the request.

Secrets Manager invokes the Lambda function with the following JSON request structure of parameters:

```
1 {
2   "Step" : "request.type",
3   "SecretId" : "string",
4   "ClientRequestToken" : "string"
5 }
```

The parameters of the request are described as follows:

- **Step** – Specifies which part of the rotation function's behavior to invoke. Each of the different values identifies a step of the rotation process. The following section The Steps of the Lambda Rotation Function explains each step in detail. The separation into independently invoked steps enables the AWS Secrets Manager team to add additional functionality in the future that might need to occur between steps.
- **secretId** – The ID or Amazon Resource Name (ARN) for the secret that you want to rotate. Every secret is assigned an ARN when you initially create it. The version that's rotated is automatically the "default" version that's labeled `AWSCURRENT`.
- **clientRequestToken** – A string that Secrets Manager provides to the Lambda function. You must pass it in turn to any Secrets Manager APIs that you call from within the Lambda function. Secrets Manager uses this token to ensure the idempotency of requests during any required retries (caused by failures of individual calls). This value is a UUID-type value to ensure uniqueness within the specified secret. This value becomes the `SecretVersionId` of the new version of the secret.

Every step is invoked with the same `secretId` and `clientTokenRequest`. Only the `Step` parameter changes with each call. This helps prevent you from having to store any state between steps. Everything you should need to know is available either in those parameters—or as part of the information in the versions that are accessed with the `AWSPENDING` or `AWSCURRENT` labels.

For descriptions of the specific tasks that should be performed in each step for the different rotation strategies, see the following topics:

- Rotating AWS Secrets Manager Secrets for One User with a Single Password
- Rotating AWS Secrets Manager Secrets by Alternating Between Two Existing Users
- Rotating AWS Secrets Manager Secrets For One User that Supports Multiple Credentials

## The Steps of the Lambda Rotation Function

The functionality that's built into the Lambda rotation function is broken into distinct steps. Each step is invoked by calling the function with one of the `Step` parameter values.

In this release of Secrets Manager, the steps are called automatically in sequence. As soon as one step ends, Secrets Manager immediately calls the Lambda function to invoke the next step.

When you specify that a secret is for one of the supported Amazon RDS databases, Secrets Manager still uses a standard Lambda function to rotate the secret. But Secrets Manager provides the Lambda function. You don't have to write it. You can, however, modify it to meet your organization's specific rotation requirements.

## The createSecret Step

In this step, the Lambda function generates a new version of the secret. Depending on your scenario, this can be as simple as just generating a new password. Or you can generate values for a completely new set of credentials, including a user name and password that are appropriate for the secured resource. These values are then stored as a new version of the secret in Secrets Manager. Other values in the secret that don't need to change, such as the connection details, are cloned from the existing version of the secret. The new version of the secret is then given the staging label `AWSPENDING` to mark it as the "in-process" version of the secret.

## The setSecret Step

In this step, the rotation function retrieves the version of the secret labeled `AWSPENDING` from Secrets Manager (the version you just created in the previous step). It then invokes the database's or service's identity service to change the existing password, or to create new credentials that match the new ones in the secret. If a new user is created, then the function must clone the permissions from the previous user. This is so that the new user can continue to perform as needed within your custom app.

To change a password or to create new credentials in the database's or service's authentication system, you must give the Lambda function permission to carry out such tasks. These are considered "administrative" tasks that require permissions that you typically don't want your users do to have. So we recommend that you use a *second* set of credentials that have permissions to change the password or create new users for the 'main' secret, as dictated by your rotation strategy. We refer to these credentials as the *master secret*, and they're stored as a separate secret from the main secret. The ARN of this master secret is stored in the main secret for use by the rotation function. The master secret never needs to be accessed by your end user custom application. It's instead accessed only by the Lambda rotation function of the main secret, to update or create new credentials in the database when rotation occurs.

## The testSecret Step

This step of the Lambda function verifies that the `AWSPENDING` version of the secret is good by trying to use it to access the secured resource in the same way that your custom application would. If the application needs read-only access to the database, then the function should verify that the test reads succeed. If the app needs to be able to write to the database, then the function should perform some test writes of some sort to verify that level of access.

## The finishSecret Step

This step performs any resource-specific finalization on this version of the secret. When it's done, the last step is for the Lambda function to move the label `AWSCURRENT` from it's current version to this new version of the secret so that your clients start using it. You can also remove the `AWSPENDING` label, but it's not technically required. At this point, the basic rotation is done. The new version of the secret is the one used by all of your clients. The old version gets the `AWSPREVIOUS` staging label, and is available for recovery as the "last known good" version of the secret, if needed. The old version that had the `AWSPREVIOUS` staging label no longer has any staging labels attached, so it's considered deprecated and subject to deletion by Secrets Manager.

# Rotating AWS Secrets Manager Secrets for One User with a Single Password

You can configure AWS Secrets Manager to automatically rotate the secret for a secured resource. In this topic, we describe how to configure rotation for a system that allows you to create a single user with a single password. You're allowed to change the password for that user when needed. This scenario is the simplest, but it isn't the most highly available solution. Clients can continue to access the secured resource while the password change is in progress. This can possibly result in some "access denied" situations.

The risk is because of the time lag that can occur between the change of the actual password and the change in the corresponding secret that tells the client which password to use. This risk can increase if the secured resource is hosted on a "server farm" where the password change takes time to propagate to all member servers. However, with an appropriate retry strategy, this risk can be significantly mitigated.

This scenario is a common one for services that are owned by someone other than the user who is accessing the service. The owner of the service lets the customer create *one* user account—often with something like the user's email address as the user name itself, or at least as a uniqueness key. The service typically allows the user to change the password as often as is required. But, it doesn't allow the user to create additional users or to change the user name.

## How Rotation Uses Labels to Manage a Single User with Changing Passwords

The following explains this scenario in more detail:

1. The scenario begins with an app that's accessing the secured resource (the database) by using the credentials stored in a secret that has a single version "A". This A version of the secret has the staging label AWSCURRENT attached. The app retrieves the secret by requesting the version with the staging label AWSCURRENT (steps 1 and 2 in the following graphic). The app then uses the credentials in that version of the secret to access the database (step 3) to retrieve the data it needs (step 4).

2. The secret rotation process creates a new version "B" of the secret (not a new secret, a new version of the same secret). This secret version B initially has the staging label AWSPENDING attached by the rotation process. Secret version B gets a new generated password. As soon as the secret is successfully stored, the rotation process changes the password for the user in the database's authentication system. It's at this point, between changing the password on the database and moving the label to the new version of the secret, that client sign-on failures can occur in step 4. Because of this risk, it's vital that the rotation process immediately proceed to the next step.

3. Because the live password is now the one stored in secret version B, the rotation process moves the `AWSCURRENT` staging label from the A version to the new B version of the secret. This also automatically moves the `AWSPREVIOUS` staging label to the version that previously had the `AWSCURRENT` staging label. This allows it to act as "last known good" in case there's a need for recovery.

4. The next request from the custom app now gets the B version of the secret because B now has the `AWSCURRENT` label. At this point, the customer app is dependent upon the new version of the secret.

## Configuring Rotation to Change Passwords Only

To configure a rotation mechanism for an authentication system that allows you to have only one user, follow the steps in this procedure:

**To configure rotation for password-only rotation**

1. Create the single user in the authentication system that protects the secured resource. Make note of the password that you set.

2. Create a Secrets Manager secret to store the details of the credentials that you created in the previous step:

    1. Sign in to the Secrets Manager console at https://console.aws.amazon.com/secretsmanager/.

    2. Choose **New secret**.

    3. For **Select secret type**, choose the option that best fits your service. Then configure the details for your database or service, including the user name and the initial password.

    4. For **AWS KMS Encryption Key**, choose the customer master key (CMK) that you want to use to encrypt this secret, or leave it set to the **DefaultMasterKey** for the account. To use the default key, the credentials that access the secret must be from the same account that owns the secret. If

the user's credentials are from a different account, then you must create and specify the Amazon Resource Namer (ARN) of a custom CMK.

5. For **Select rotation period**, choose or type the number of days between rotations. **Note** When you use the Secrets Manager console to configure rotation, by default, expiration is automatically enabled and set to the number of days in a rotation cycle + 7.

6. For **What credentials can rotation this secret?**, choose **Use the same credentials**. **Note** This example scenario assumes that the user is allowed to change their own password, and that you can't use a second user with permissions to change the password on the first user.

7. Choose **Next step**.

8. Type a **Secret name** and optional **Description**. You can also choose to add tags if you want to.

9. Choose **Store secret**.

3. Examine your new secret to get the ARN of the Lambda rotation function.

   1. On the **Secrets** list page, choose the name of the secret that you created in step 2.

   2. In the Secret details / Secret rotation section, choose the ARN of the rotation function to open it in Lambda.

   3. Customize the rotation function to meet your specific requirements. You can use the following requirements for each step as the basis for writing the function.

      - **createSecret step**:
        - Retrieve the `AWSCURRENT` version of the secret by using the `GetSecretValue` operation.
        - Extract the protected secret text from the `SecureString` field, and store it in a structure that you can modify.
        - Generate a new password by using an algorithm that generates passwords with the maximum length and complexity requirements that are supported by the protected resource.
        - Overwrite the `password` field in the structure with the new one that you generated in the previous step. Keep all other details, such as `username` and the connection details the same.
        - Store the modified copy of the secret structure by passing it as the `SecureString` parameter in a call to `PutSecretValue`. The new version of the secret is labeled `AWSPENDING`.
      - **setSecret step**:
        - Retrieve the `AWSPENDING` version of the secret by using the `GetSecretValue` operation.
        - Issue commands to the secured resource's authentication system to change the existing user's password to the one stored in the new `AWSPENDING` version of the secret.
      - **testSecret step**:
        - Retrieve the `AWSPENDING` version of the secret by using the `GetSecretValue` operation.
        - Issue commands to the secured resource to attempt to access it by using the credentials in the secret.
      - **finishSecret step**:
        - Move the label `AWSCURRENT` to the version labeled `AWSPENDING`. This automatically also moves the staging label `AWSPREVIOUS` to the secret that you just removed `AWSCURRENT` from.
        - (Optional) Remove the label `AWSPENDING` from its version of the secret.

**Important**

Remember that in this scenario, there's no opportunity for your users to continue operating with the old version while you create and verify the new version. Therefore, between the time in the `setSecret` phase when you change the password, and the time in the `finishSecret` phase when you move the `AWSCURRENT` label to the new version, it's possible for your clients to use the wrong credentials and get access denied errors. Be sure to include reasonable retry functionality in your client app for this situation to help mitigate this risk.

# Rotating AWS Secrets Manager Secrets by Alternating Between Two Existing Users

You can configure AWS Secrets Manager to automatically rotate the secret for a secured resource.

In this topic, we describe how to configure rotation for a system that allows you to create and alternate between two users that you can change the password for, when needed. This enables you to remove the potential for downtime that occurs in the scenario where you're limited to only one user account. In this case, you change more than just the password in a secret version. Each version must also capture the change in the user, and alternate between each user with each rotation cycle.

If the administrator enables you to create a third "master" user with the elevated permissions to change the password for the first two users, we recommend that you do so. This is more secure than allowing the users to have permissions to change their own passwords. If you do configure the scenario this way, then you need to create a second secret that's used to change the password of the users that are alternated in the first secret. Create that "master" secret first, so that it's available to reference when you configure the "user" secret.

The scenario (described in the following section), which is implemented by the templates that are provided by Secrets Manager, deactivates the current credentials, but doesn't immediately delete them. Instead, the version of the secret with those credentials is marked with the staging label AWSPREVIOUS. This preserves those credentials for one additional rotation cycle as the "last known good" credentials. They are then available for recovery if something happens to the current credentials.

The credentials are only truly removed after the second rotation cycle when the user is brought back into active service, as described later in this topic. This means that if you want a given set of credentials to only be valid for a given number of days, we recommend that you set the rotation period to one-half of that minus one. This allows the two rotation cycles to both complete and the credentials to become fully deprecated within the specified time frame.

For example, if you have a compliance-mandated maximum credential lifetime of 90 days, then we recommend that you set your rotation interval to 44 days (90/2 - 1 = 44). At day 0, the new credentials are created in a rotation and are stage labeled as AWSCURRENT. On day 44, the next rotation demotes the secret with those credentials to AWSPREVIOUS, and clients stop actively using them. On day 88, the next rotation removes all staging labels from the version. The version is fully deprecated at this point and the user on the database is recycled with a new password, which starts the cycle over again.

## How Rotation Uses Labels to Alternate Between Two Users

Using staging labels makes it possible to switch back and forth between two users. One, labeled AWSCURRENT, is actively used by the clients. When rotation is triggered, the rotation process assigns a new password to the inactive second user. Those credentials are stored in a new version of the secret. After verifying that access with the credentials in the new secret version works, the rotation process moves the AWSCURRENT label to the new version, which makes it the active version. The next time the rotation cycle is triggered, the roles of the two user accounts are reversed.

**Basic Example Scenario**

The following explains this scenario in more detail:

1. The scenario begins with an app that's accessing the database by using a secret that has a single version "A". This A version of the secret has the label AWSCURRENT attached and contains credentials for the first of the two users. The app retrieves the secret by requesting the version labeled AWSCURRENT (steps 1 and 2 in the following graphic). The app then uses the credentials in that version of the secret to access the database (step 3) to retrieve the data it needs (step 4).

2. During the very first rotation, the process creates a new "B" version of the secret (not a new secret, a new version of the same secret). It basically clones all details of the A version, except that it switches the user name to the second user and generates a new password. Then the rotation process updates the second user with this new password. This secret version B initially has the label `AWSPENDING`, which is attached by the rotation process. Because the custom app is programmed to always request the `AWSCURRENT` label and that hasn't yet moved, the app continues to retrieve and use the original A version of the secret for credentials to access the database.

3. After testing the version B secret to ensure it works, the rotation process moves the `AWSCURRENT` label from the A version, and attaches it to the new B version of the secret. This also automatically moves the `AWSPREVIOUS` staging label to the version that previously had the `AWSCURRENT` staging label. This allows it to act as "last known good" in case there's a need for recovery. The `AWSPREVIOUS` version of the secret continues to be available for recovery for one additional rotation cycle. It will be truly deprecated when it's reused in the cycle that follows.

4. The next request from the custom app now gets the B version of the secret because B now has the `AWSCURRENT` label. The customer app is now using the second user with its new password to access the database.

## Configuring Rotation to Switch Between Two Users

If your secret is for one of the supported Amazon RDS databases, follow the procedures in Enabling Rotation for an Amazon RDS Database Secret.

If instead you want to configure rotation for another service or database, create your Lambda rotation function and customize it using these instructions:

1. Create two users in your database or service. Make note of the user names and passwords that you use. Make sure that each user has the ability to change their own password.

2. Create a secret that contains the credentials of the first user.

Follow the steps at Rotating AWS Secrets Manager Secrets for Other Databases or Services to create a generic Lambda rotation function template that you can customize. When you get to step 7, customize your function by using the following information.

Use the following logic as the basis for writing your rotation function:

- **createSecret phase:**
  - Retrieve the `AWSCURRENT` version of the secret by using the `GetSecretValue` operation.
  - Extract the protected secret text from the `SecretString` field, and place it in a structure that you can manipulate.
  - Look at the `username` field and determine what the alternate user name is.
  - Determine whether a user with the alternate user name exists on the database. If it doesn't, this must be the first time through the rotation process. Clone the current user and its permissions.
  - Set the `username` entry in the copy of the secret's structure to the alternate user name.
  - Generate a new password with the maximum length and complexity requirements that are supported by the protected resource.
  - Set the `password` entry in the copy of the secret's structure to the new password.
  - Store the modified copy of the structure into the secret by passing it as the `SecureString` parameter in a call to `PutSecretValue`. The new version of the secret is labeled `AWSPENDING`.
- **setSecret phase:**
  - Retrieve the `AWSPENDING` version of the secret by using the `GetSecretValue` operation.
  - Extract the user name and password from the `SecureString` field.
  - Issue commands to the secured resource's authentication system to change the specified user's password to that value.
- **testSecret phase:**
  - Retrieve the `AWSPENDING` version of the secret by using the `GetSecretValue` operation.
  - Issue commands to the secured resource to attempt to access it by using the credentials in the secret.
- **finishSecret phase:**
  - Move the label `AWSCURRENT` to the version with the label `AWSPENDING`.
  - (Optional) Remove the label `AWSPENDING` from its version of the secret.

**Note**
In this scenario, there's less chance of users getting an error during the rotation of the secret. They continue to use the old version, while you configure the new version. Only when the new version is tested and ready do you switch the label to point to the new version and the clients start using it. However, because some servers are in farms with propagation delays when changing passwords, you should ensure that you include a reasonable delay (most likely in the **setSecret** step before you test) to ensure that the password has had time to be propagated to all servers. Also, be sure to include reasonable retry functionality in your client app for this situation, to help mitigate this risk.

# Rotating AWS Secrets Manager Secrets For One User that Supports Multiple Credentials

You can configure AWS Secrets Manager to automatically rotate the secret for a secured resource. In this topic, we describe how to configure rotation for an authentication system that allows you to create a single user with at least two credential sets.

As a best practice, we recommend that you set up a second "master" secret to store the credentials of a different user that has permissions to delete and create credentials for the main user. This enables you to limit the permissions that you grant to the main user to only those required by your application. And it offloads the administrative tasks to the second user, which the end users don't have any access to. The second user is accessed only by the rotation function of the main secret to delete the old access key and create a new one.

## How Rotation Uses Labels to Manage a Single User with Multiple Credentials

The following example explains this scenario in more detail. It uses the example of a service that enables a user to have two separate "API keys" that are generated by the service and don't need to be generated by your rotation function:

1. The scenario begins with an app that's accessing the secured resource (the database) by using one of the API keys stored in a secret that has a single version "A". This A version of the secret has the staging label `AWSCURRENT` attached. The app retrieves the secret by requesting the version with the staging label `AWSCURRENT` (steps 1 and 2 in the following graphic). The app then uses the API key in that version of the secret to access the database (step 3) to retrieve the data it needs (step 4).

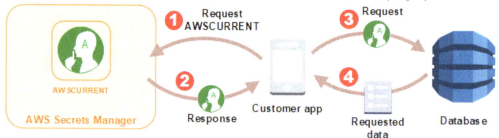

2. The secret rotation function deletes the API key that isn't currently referenced by secret version "A", and creates a new API key for the same user. The rotation function then creates a new "B" version of the secret (not a new secret, a new version of the same secret). It basically clones the details from the "A" version, except that it replaces the API key details with those from the newly created API key. This secret version "B" initially has the staging label `AWSPENDING` attached by the rotation process. Because the custom app is programmed to always request the `AWSCURRENT` label and that hasn't yet moved, the app continues to retrieve and use the original A version of the secret, for the API key to access the secured resource.

3. After testing the "B" version of the secret to ensure that it works, the rotation process moves the `AWSCURRENT` label from the "A" version and attaches it to the new "B" version of the secret. This also automatically moves `AWSPREVIOUS` staging label to the version that had previously had the `AWSCURRENT` staging label.

This allows it to act as "last known good" in case there's a need for recovery.

4. The next request from the custom app now gets the "B" version of the secret because "B" now has the AWSCURRENT label. At this point, the customer app is using the API key in the new version of the secret. When the next rotation cycle occurs, the "B" version of the secret becomes the "A" version, and you start again in step a (earlier in this section).

## Configuring Rotation to Alternate Credentials for a User

To configure a rotation mechanism for an authentication system that allows you to have only one user, follow the steps in this procedure:

**To configure rotation for a user that has two sets of credentials**

1. Create your user in the authentication system that protects the secured resource. Make note of the user name and credentials that you set. For this discussion, we'll refer to them as **Creds1** and **Creds2**.

2. Create one Secrets Manager secret to store the details of the credentials that you created in the previous step. This secret initially holds Creds1 for the user:

    1. Sign in to the Secrets Manager console at https://console.aws.amazon.com/secretsmanager/.

    2. Choose **New secret**.

    3. For **Select secret type**, choose **Other type of secret**, including the user name and the first set of credentials. For example, enter two key-value pairs for the protected secret text. They could look something like:
    [See the AWS documentation website for more details]

    4. For **AWS KMS Encryption Key**, choose the key you want to use to encrypt this secret, or leave the default set to the **DefaultMasterKey** for the account. To use the default key, the credentials that access the secret must be from the same account that owns the secret. If the user's credentials are from a different account, then you must create and specify a custom customer master key (CMK).

    5. For **Select rotation period**, choose or type the number of days between rotations. **Note** When you use the Secrets Manager console to configure rotation, by default, expiration is automatically enabled and set to the number of days between rotations + 7.

    6. For **Select the Lambda rotation function**, choose **Create function**.

    7. Choose **Next step**.

8. Type a **Secret name** and optional **Description**. You can also choose to add tags if you want to.

9. Choose **Store secret**.

3. Examine your new secret to get the Amazon Resource Name (ARN) of the Lambda rotation function.

1. On the **Secrets** list page, choose the name of the secret that you created in step 2.

2. In the Secret details / Secret rotation section, choose the ARN of the rotation function to open it in Lambda.

3. Use the following logic as the basis for writing your rotation function:

- **createSecret step**:
  - Retrieve the `AWSCURRENT` version of the secret by using the `GetSecretValue` operation.
  - Extract the `SecureString` value from the secret and store it in a structure that you can modify.
  - Determine which API key isn't the one that's referenced in the `AWSCURRENT` version of the secret.
  - Issue commands to the service to delete the API key that you determined in the previous step.
  - Issue commands to the service to create a new access key for the same user.
  - Overwrite the API key and its identifier in the copy of the secret's structure with those from the new API key that you just created. Keep all other details the same.
  - Store the modified copy of the protected secret text by passing it as the `SecureString` parameter in a call to `PutSecretValue`. The new version of the secret is labeled `AWSPENDING`.
- **setSecret step**:
  - The setSecret step in this scenario doesn't do anything. The API key is created in the `createSecret` step, because you must have the API key and its identifier to store in the secret. You don't generate your own key like you do for most other scenarios.
- **testSecret step**:
  - Retrieve the `AWSPENDING` version of the secret by using the `GetSecretValue` operation.
  - Issue commands to the secured resource to attempt to access it by using the API key that's in this version of the secret.
- **finishSecret step**:
  - Move the label `AWSCURRENT` to the version labeled `AWSPENDING`. This automatically also moves the staging label `AWSPREVIOUS` to the secret that you just removed `AWSCURRENT` from.
  - (Optional) Remove the label `AWSPENDING` from its version of the secret.

# Deleting Lambda Rotation Functions That You No Longer Need

After you create a rotation function for a secret, the time will come when that secret is no longer needed. Deleting the secret is an obvious step. However, you might also want to consider removing the Lambda rotation function that rotates the secret. If you share the rotation function among several secrets, then, of course, you don't want to delete the function until you delete the last secret rotated by the function.

If you create the function as described in this guide, by using AWS Serverless Application Repository template, then you don't simply delete the function. Secrets Manager created the function as part of an AWS CloudFormation stack. Deleting the stack deletes everything that the stack created. In this case, it's both the Lambda function and the IAM role that grants permissions to the function. You must perform the following steps to delete everything cleanly.

**To delete a rotation function that you created with an AWS Serverless Application Repository template**
Follow the steps under one of the following tabs:

---

**[ Using the AWS Management Console ]**

**Minimum permissions**
To delete a Lambda rotation function that you created by using one of the AWS Serverless Application Repository templates, you must have the permissions that are required to navigate to your stack and delete all of its created components:
cloudformation:ListStacks cloudformation:DescribeStack cloudformation:ListStackResources cloudformation:DeleteStack lambda:ListFunctions lambda:GetFunction lambda:DeleteFunction iam:ListRoles iam:DetachRolePolicy iam:DeleteRolePolicy iam:DeleteRole cloudformation:DeleteStack You can grant all of these by attaching the following AWS managed policies:
SecretsManagerReadWrite IAMFullAccess

1. Open the AWS Lambda console at https://console.aws.amazon.com/lambda/.

2. Navigate to the list of functions, and choose the name of the function that you want to delete.

3. On the function's details page, a banner at the top says This function belongs to the CloudFormation stack aws-serverless-repository-SecretsManager*<rotation_template_name><unique_guid>*. **Visit the CloudFormation console to manage this stack.**.

   Choose the **CloudFormation console** link to open the AWS CloudFormation console on that stack's details page.

4. If you added any inline permission policies to the IAM role (instead of editing the existing inline policies), or if you attached any additional managed policies, then you must delete or detach those policies before AWS CloudFormation can delete the stack:

   1. Expand the **Resources** section for the stack, and then choose the **Physical ID** value for the row, with the **Type** set to **AWS::IAM::Role**. This opens the IAM console in a separate tab.

   2. Examine the rows with **Inline policy** as the **Policy type**. You should see the AWSLambdaBasicExecutionRole AWS managed function attached. You should also see one or two inline policies named SecretsManagerPolicy0 and SecretsManagerPolicy1. If there are any policies other than those, they were not created as part of the stack. They were added manually after the stack was created. You must manually delete or detach them. If you don't, the request to delete the stack in the following steps can fail.

   3. Return to the **Stack Detail** page of the AWS CloudFormation console.

5. Choose **Other Actions**, and then choose **Delete Stack**.

6. On the **Delete Stack** confirmation dialog box, choose **Yes, Delete**.

   The **Status** changes to **DELETE_IN_PROGRESS**. If the deletion is successful, it eventually changes to **DELETE_COMPLETE**.

7. When you return to the list of stacks, the one you just deleted is no longer present.

---

### [ Using the AWS CLI or SDK Operations ]

### Minimum permissions

To delete a Lambda rotation function that you created by using one of the AWS Serverless Application Repository templates, you must have the permissions required to perform each of the AWS CLI or equivalent API operations that are listed in the following steps. You can grant all of these by attaching the following two AWS managed policies:
SecretsManagerReadWrite IAMFullAccess

1. Open a command prompt where you can run the AWS CLI commands.

2. To determine which AWS CloudFormation stack contains a specific function, run the following command with the function name passed as the `--physical-resource-id` parameter. This results in a list of resources that are associated with the stack that owns the specified function.

```
 1 $ aws cloudformation describe-stack-resources --physical-resource-id
     MyLambdaRotationFunction
 2 {{
 3     "StackResources": [
 4         {
 5             "StackName": "aws-serverless-repository-MyLambdaCreationStack",
 6             "StackId": "arn:aws:cloudformation:us-east-1:123456789012:stack/aws-serverless-
                 repository-MyLambdaCreationStack/EXAMPLE2-90ab-cdef-fedc-ba987EXAMPLE",
 7             "LogicalResourceId": "SecretsManagerRotationTemplate",
 8             "PhysicalResourceId": "MySecretsManagerRotationFunction",
 9             "ResourceType": "AWS::Lambda::Function",
10             "Timestamp": "2018-04-27T18:03:05.490Z",
11             "ResourceStatus": "CREATE_COMPLETE"
12         },
13         {
14             "StackName": "aws-serverless-repository-MyLambdaCreationStack",
15             "StackId": "arn:aws:cloudformation:us-east-1:123456789012:stack/aws-serverless-
                 repository-MyLambdaCreationStack/EXAMPLE2-90ab-cdef-fedc-ba987EXAMPLE",
16             "LogicalResourceId": "SecretsManagerRotationTemplateRole",
17             "PhysicalResourceId": "aws-serverless-repository-SecretsManagerRotationTe-<
                 random-chars>",
18             "ResourceType": "AWS::IAM::Role",
19             "Timestamp": "2018-04-27T18:03:00.623Z",
20             "ResourceStatus": "CREATE_COMPLETE"
21         }
22     ]
23 }
```

3. We're initially interested in the `StackId` and `PhysicalResourceId` response values that are associated with the "ResourceType" :"AWS::IAM::Role". This is the name of the IAM role that has permissions to invoke the function. If you added any inline permission policies to the IAM role (instead of editing the existing inline policies), or if you attached any additional managed policies, then you must delete or detach those policies before AWS CloudFormation can delete the stack.

To determine if there are any embedded inline policies, run the following command.

```
1 $ aws iam list-role-policies --role-name <role-name-from-PhysicalResourceId-on-previous-
    command>
2 {
3     "PolicyNames": [
4         "SecretsManagerRotationTemplateRolePolicy0",
5         "SecretsManagerRotationTemplateRolePolicy1"
6     ]
7 }
```

The inline policies that are named as shown here are expected, and you don't need to do anything with them.

4. If there are any policies listed other than those two, you must delete them from the role before you can proceed.

```
1 $ aws iam delete-role-policy --role-name <role-name-from-PhysicalResourceId-on-previous-
    command> /
2         --policy-name <policy-name-from-previous-command>
```

5. Now check to see if there are any managed policies that are attached to the role:

```
1 $ aws iam list-attached-role-policies --role-name <role-name-from-PhysicalResourceId-on-
    previous-command>
```

6. If there are any policies listed at all in the previous command's output, run this final preparatory command to detach them from the role:

```
1 $ aws iam detach-role-policy --role-name <role-name-from-PhysicalResourceId-on-previous-
    command> /
2         --policy-arn <ARN-of-policy-discovered-in-previous-command>
```

7. Now you can delete the stack, which deletes all of its resources. Pass the name of the stack that you retrieved in step 2 as the --stack-name:

```
1 $ aws cloudformation delete-stack --stack-name aws-serverless-repository-
    MyLambdaCreationStack
```

Both the IAM role and the Lambda rotation function are deleted shortly after this command runs.

---

# Authentication and Access Control for AWS Secrets Manager

Access to AWS Secrets Manager requires AWS credentials. Those credentials must have permissions to access the AWS resources that you want to access, such as your Secrets Manager secrets. The following sections provide details on how you can use AWS Identity and Access Management (IAM) policies to help secure access to your secrets and control who can access and administer them.

Because secrets are, by definition, extremely sensitive information, access to your secrets must be tightly controlled. Using the permissions capabilities of AWS and IAM permission policies, you can tightly control which users (or services) have access to your secrets. You can specify which API, CLI, and console operations the user can perform on the authorized secrets. By taking advantage of the granular access features in the policy language, you can choose to limit the user to only a subset of your secrets or even to one individual secret by using tags as filters. You can also restrict a user to specific versions of a secret by using staging labels attached to the versions as filters.

You can also determine who can *manage* which secrets. You can determine who can update or modify the secrets and their associated metadata. If you have admin (all, sometimes called */* meaning "all actions on all resources") permissions to the AWS Secrets Manager service, you can delegate access to Secrets Manager tasks by granting permissions to others.

You can attach the policies to your users, groups, and roles and specify what secrets the attached identities can access. Those policies specify what actions each principal can perform on which secrets.

For general information about IAM permissions policies, see Overview of IAM Policies in the *IAM User Guide*.

For the permissions available specifically for use with AWS Secrets Manager, see Actions, Resources, and Context Keys You Can Use in an IAM Policy for AWS Secrets Manager

The following sections describe how to manage permissions for AWS Secrets Manager. We recommend that you read the overview first.

- Overview of Managing Access Permissions to Your AWS Secrets Manager Secrets
- Using Identity-Based Policies (IAM Policies) for AWS Secrets Manager

# Overview of Managing Access Permissions to Your AWS Secrets Manager Secrets

All AWS resources, including the secrets you store in AWS Secrets Manager, are owned by an AWS account, and the permissions to create or access those resources are governed by permissions policies. An account administrator can control access to AWS resources by attaching permissions policies to the IAM identities (users, groups, and roles) that need to access the resources.

**Note**
An *administrator* (or administrator user) is a user who has administrator permissions. This typically means that they have permissions to perform all operations on all resources for a service. For more information, see IAM Best Practices in the *IAM User Guide*.

An admin for AWS Secrets Manager in an account can perform administrative tasks, including delegating admin permissions to other IAM users or roles in the account. To do this, you attach an IAM permissions policy to an IAM user, group, or role. By default, a user has no permissions at all; this results in what is commonly referred to as an *implicit deny*. The policy you attach overrides the implicit deny with an *explicit allow* that specifies which actions the user can perform, and which resources they can perform the actions on. The policy can be attached to users, groups, and roles within the account. If the permissions are granted to a role, that role can be assumed by users in other accounts in the organization.

**Topics**
- Authentication
- Access Control (Authorization)

## Authentication

Authentications is the process of establishing an identity that represents you in the services that you access. Typically, an identity is assigned to you and you access it by proving that you are who you say your are. You do this by supplying "credentials" with your request, such as a user name and password, or by encrypting your request with an AWS access key.

AWS supports the following types of identities:

- **AWS account root user** – When you sign up for AWS, you provide an email address and password for your AWS account. These are your *root credentials* and they provide complete access to all of your AWS resources. **Important**
  For security reasons, we recommend that you use the root credentials only to create an administrator user, which is an IAM user with full permissions to your AWS account. Then you can use this administrator user to create other IAM users and roles with limited, job-role specific permissions. For more information, see Create Individual IAM Users (IAM Best Practices) and Creating An Admin User and Group in the *IAM User Guide*.

- **IAM user** – An IAM user is an identity within your AWS account that has specific permissions (for example, to access an AWS Secrets Manager secret). You can use an IAM user name and password to sign in to secure AWS webpages like the AWS Management Console, AWS Discussion Forums, or the AWS Support Center.

  In addition to a user name and password, you can also create access keys for each user to enable the user to access AWS services programmatically, through one of the AWS SDKsor the command line tools. The SDKs and command line tools use the access keys to cryptographically sign API requests. If you don't use the AWS tools, you must sign API requests yourself. AWS KMS supports *Signature Version 4*, an AWS protocol for authenticating API requests. For more information about authenticating API requests, see Signature Version 4 Signing Process in the *AWS General Reference*.

- **IAM role** – An IAM role is another IAM identity you can create in your account that has specific permissions. It is similar to an IAM user, but it is not associated with a specific person. An IAM role enables you to obtain temporary access keys to access AWS services and resources programmatically. AWS roles are useful in the following situations:
    - **Federated user access** – Instead of creating an IAM user, you can use preexisting user identities from AWS Directory Service, your enterprise user directory, or a web identity provider. These are known as *federated users*. Federated users are associated with IAM roles by an identity provider. For more information about federated users, see Federated Users and Roles in the *IAM User Guide*.
    - **Cross-account access** – You can use an IAM role in your AWS account to allow another AWS account permissions to access your account's resources. For an example, see Tutorial: Delegate Access Across AWS Accounts Using IAM Roles in the *IAM User Guide*.
    - **AWS service access** – You can use an IAM role in your account to allow an AWS service permissions to access your account's resources. For example, you can create a role that allows Amazon Redshift to access an S3 bucket on your behalf and then load data stored in the S3 bucket into an Amazon Redshift cluster. For more information, see Creating a Role to Delegate Permissions to an AWS Service in the *IAM User Guide*.
    - **Applications running on EC2 instances** – Instead of storing access keys on an EC2 instance for use by applications that run on the instance and make AWS API requests, you can use an IAM role to provide temporary access keys for these applications. To assign an IAM role to an EC2 instance, you create an *instance profile* and then attach it when you launch the instance. An instance profile contains the role and enables applications running on the EC2 instance to get temporary access keys. For more information, see Using Roles for Applications on Amazon EC2 in the *IAM User Guide*.

After you sign in with an identity you then use access control (authorization) to establish what you (through your identity) are allowed to do.

## Access Control (Authorization)

You can have a valid identity with credentials to authenticate your requests, but you also need *permissions* to make AWS Secrets Manager API requests to create, manage, or use Secrets Manager resources. For example, you must have permissions to create a secret, to manage the secret, to retrieve the secret, and so on. The following pages describe how to manage permissions for AWS Secrets Manager.

### Secrets Manager Policies: Combining Resources and Actions

This section discusses how AWS Secrets Manager concepts map to their IAM equivalent concepts.

### Policies

Permissions in AWS Secrets Manager, as in almost all AWS services, are granted by creating and attaching permission policies. Policies come in two basic types:

- **Identity-based policies** – these are attached directly to a user, group, or role. The policy specifies what the attached identity is allowed to do. The attached user is automatically and implicitly the `Principal` of the policy. You can specify the `Actions` that the identity can perform, and the `Resources` the identity can perform the actions on. They enable you to:
    - Grant access to multiple resources that you want to share with the identity.
    - Control access to APIs for resources that don't yet exist, such as the various `Create*` operations.
    - Grant access to an IAM group to a resource.
- **Resource-based policies** – these are attached directly to a resource, in this case, a secret. The policy specifies who can access the secret and what actions they can perform against it. The attached secret is automatically and implicitly the `Resource` of the policy. You can specify the `Principals` that can access the secret and the `Actions` that the principals can perform. They enable you to:

- Grant access to multiple principals (users or roles) to a single secret. Note that you *can't* specify an IAM group as a principal in a resource-based policy. Only users and roles are principals.
- Grant access to users or roles in other AWS accounts by specifying the account IDs in the `Principal` element of a policy statement. A requirement for this "cross account" access to a secret is one of the primary reasons to use a resource-based policy.

**Note**
At this time, Secrets Manager supports only identity-based policies.

### Resources

In AWS Secrets Manager, **secrets** are the resources you can control access to.

Each secret has a unique Amazon Resource Name (ARN) associated with it. You can control access to a secret by specifying its ARN in the `Resource` element of an IAM permission policy. The ARN of a secret looks like the following:

```
1 arn:aws:secretsmanager:<region>:<account-id>:secret:optional-path/secret-name-6-random-
    characters
```

### Understanding Resource Ownership

The AWS account owns the resources that you create in the account, regardless of who created the resources. Specifically, the resource owner is the AWS account of the root user, IAM user, or IAM role whose credentials authenticate the resource creation request. The following examples illustrate how this works:

- If you sign in as the root user account to create a secret, your AWS account is the owner of the resource .
- If you create an IAM user in your account and grant permissions to create a secret to that user, the user can create a secret. However, the AWS account to which the user belongs, owns the secret.
- If you create an IAM role in your account with permissions to create a secret, anyone who can assume the role can create a secret. The AWS account to which the role (not the assuming user) belongs, owns the secret.

### Actions & Operations

AWS Secrets Manager provides a set of *operations* (API calls and CLI commands) to work with secrets. They enable you to do things like create, list, access, modify, or delete secrets. These operations correspond to policy *actions* that you can use to grant or deny access to that operation. Most of the time, there is a one-to-one relationship between API operations and the actions you can assign in a policy. To control access to an operation, specify its corresponding action in the `Action` element of an IAM policy. For a list of Secrets Manager actions that can be used in a policy, see Actions, Resources, and Context Keys You Can Use in an IAM Policy for AWS Secrets Manager.

When you combine both an `Action` element and a `Resource` element in an identity-based permission policy `Statement`, then you control both the actions that can be performed and the resources on which they can be performed. The limits apply to the user, group, or role to which the policy is attached.

### Managing Access to Resources with Policies

A *permissions policy* describes *who* can perform *which actions* on *which resources*. The following section explains the available options for creating permissions policies. It briefly describes the elements that make up a policy.

**Note**
This section discusses using IAM in the context of AWS Secrets Manager. It doesn't provide detailed information about the IAM service. For complete IAM documentation, see the IAM User Guide. For information about IAM policy syntax and descriptions, see the AWS IAM Policy Reference in the *IAM User Guide.*

It's important to understand that it doesn't really matter whether you use secret-based or identity-based permission policies. The results are the same. All of the policies that apply are grouped together and processed as if they were one big policy. How they interact is controlled by this basic rule structure:

| Explicit Deny » Explicit Allow » Implicit Deny (default) |
| --- |

For a request to perform an AWS operation on an AWS resource, the following rules apply:

- **If any statement in any policy with an explicit Deny matches the request's action and resource**: The explicit deny overrides everything else. The specified actions on the specified resources are always blocked.
- **If there is no explicit deny but there is a statement with an explicit Allow that matches the request's action and resource**: The explicit allow applies, granting actions in that statement access to the resources in that statement.
- **If there is no statement with an explicit deny and no statement with an explicit allow that matches the request's action and resource**: The request is *implicitly* denied by default.

It's important to understand: an *implicit* deny can be overridden with an explicit allow. An *explicit* deny can't ever be overridden.

**Effective permissions when multiple policies apply**

| Policy A | Policy B | Effective permissions |
| --- | --- | --- |
| Allows | Silent | Access allowed |
| Allows | Allows | Access allowed |
| Allows | Denies | Access denied |
| Silent | Silent | Access denied |
| Silent | Allows | Access allowed |
| Silent | Denies | Access denied |
| Denies | Silent | Access denied |
| Denies | Allows | Access denied |
| Denies | Denies | Access denied |

You can include the effect of additional policies by taking the effective permission of the first two policies (the results) and treat that like a new Policy A and then add the results of the third as Policy B, repeating for each additional policy that applies.

**Topics**

- AWS Managed Policies
- Specifying Policy Statement Elements
- Identity-based Policies

**AWS Managed Policies**

AWS addresses many common use cases by providing standalone IAM policies that are created and administered by AWS. These *managed policies* grant necessary permissions for common use cases so that you can avoid having to investigate which permissions are needed. For more information, see AWS Managed Policies in the *IAM User Guide*.

The following AWS managed policy, which you can attach to users in your account, is specific to AWS Secrets Manager:

- **SecretsManagerReadWrite**—This policy can be attached to IAM users and roles that need to administer AWS Secrets Manager. It grants full permissions to the Secrets Manager service itself, and limited permissions to other services, such as AWS KMS, Amazon CloudFront, AWS Serverless Application Repository, and AWS Lambda.

You can view this policy here: https://console.aws.amazon.com/iam/home?#/policies/arn:aws:iam::aws:policy/SecretsManagerReadWrite **Important**
For security reasons, this managed policy does *not* include the IAM permissions needed to configure rotation. You must explicitly grant the IAMFullAccess managed policy to a Secrets Manager administrator to enable them to configure rotation.

One important advantage of using an AWS managed policy is that is maintained by the Secrets Manager team. If the rotation process is ever expanded to include new functionality that requires additional permissions, those permission will be added to the managed policy at that time, and your rotation functions will automatically receive the new permissions so that they continue to operated as expected without any interruption.

### Important

For security reasons, the managed policy provided by Secrets Manager does not include the IAM permissions required to configure rotation. We recommend that you grant those permissions only to trusted individuals. Grant them by attaching both the `IAMFullAccess` managed policy and the `SecretsManagerReadWrite` managed policy.

### Specifying Policy Statement Elements

This is a very brief overview of IAM permission policies from the perspective of Secrets Manager. For more detail about IAM policy syntax, see the AWS IAM Policy Reference in the *IAM User Guide.*

AWS Secrets Manager defines a set of API operations that can interact with or manipulate a secret in some way. To grant permissions for these operations, Secrets Manager defines a set of corresponding actions that you can specify in a policy. For example, Secrets Manager defines actions that work on a secret, such as `PutSecret`, `GetSecretMetadata`, `ListSecretVersions`, and `RotateSecret`, among others.

A policy document must have a `Version` element. We recommend always using the latest version to ensure you can use all of the available features. As of this writing, the only available version is `2012-10-17` (the latest version).

In addition, a secret policy document must have one `Statement` element with one or more statements in an array, and each statement consists of up to six elements:

- **Sid** – (Optional) The `Sid` is a statement identifier, an arbitrary string you can use to identify the statement.
- **Effect** – (Required) Use this keyword to specify whether the policy statement allows or denies the action on the resource. If you don't explicitly allow access to a resource, access is *implicitly* denied. You also can explicitly deny access to a resource, which you might do to ensure that a user cannot perform the specified action on the specified resource, even if a different policy grants access. It is important to understand that when there are multiple statements that overlap, explicit deny in a statement overrides any other statements that explicitly allow. Explicit allow statements override the implicit deny that is present by default.
- **Action** – (Required) Use this keyword to identify the actions that you want to allow or deny. These actions usually, but not always, correspond one-to-one with the available operations. For example, depending on the specified `Effect`, `secretsmanager:PutSecret` either allows or denies the user permissions to perform the AWS Secrets Manager `PutSecret` operation.
- **Resource** – (Required) In an identity-based policy attached to a user, group, or role, you use this keyword to specify the Amazon Resource Name (ARN) of the resource to which the policy statement applies. If you don't want the statement to restrict access to a specific resource, then you can use "*" and the resulting statement restricts only actions.
- **Condition** – (Optional) Use this keyword to specify additional conditions that must be true for the statement to "match" and the `Effect` to apply. For more information, see IAM JSON Policy Elements: Condition.

## Identity-based Policies

You can attach policies to IAM identities. For example, you can do the following:

- **Attach a permissions policy to a user or a group in your account** – To grant a user permissions to create a secret, you can attach a permissions policy directly to the user or to a group that the user belongs to (recommended).
- **Attach a permissions policy to a role** – You can attach a permissions policy to an IAM role to grant access to a secret to anyone who assumes the role. This include users in these scenarios:
  - **Federated users** - You can grant permissions to users authenticated by an identity system other than IAM. For example, you can associate IAM roles to mobile app users who sign in using Amazon Cognito. The role grants the app temporary credentials with the permissions found in the role's permission policy. Those permissions can include access to a secret. For more information, see What is Amazon Cognito? in the *Amazon Cognito Developer Guide*.
  - **Applications running on EC2 instances** - You can grant permissions to applications running on an Amazon EC2 instance. This is done by attaching an IAM role to the instance. When an application in the instance wants to invoke an AWS API, it can get AWS temporary credentials from the instance metadata. These temporary credentials are associated with a role and limited by the role's permissions policy. Those permissions can include access to a secret.
  - **Cross-account access** - An administrator in account A can create a role to grant permissions to a user in a different account B. For example:
    1. The account A administrator creates an IAM role and attaches a permissions policy to the role that grants access to secrets in account A and specifies what users can do with them.
    2. The account A administrator attaches a trust policy to the role that identifies the account ID of B in the `Principal` element to specify who can assume the role.
    3. The account B administrator can then delegate permissions to any users in account B that enable them to assume account A's role. Doing this allows users in account B to access the secrets in the first account.

For more information about using IAM to delegate permissions, see Access Management in the *IAM User Guide*.

The following example policy can be attached to a user, group, or role and allows the affected user or role to perform the `DescribeSecret` and `GetSecretValue` operations in your account only on secrets whose path and name begins with the path "TestEnv/". The user or role is also restricted to retrieving only the version of the secret that has the staging label `AWSCURRENT` attached. Replace the and *<account_id>* placeholders in the following examples with your actual values.

```
1  {
2    "Version": "2012-10-17",
3    "Statement": [
4      {
5        "Sid" : "Stmt1DescribeSecret",
6        "Effect": "Allow",
7        "Action": [ "secretsmanager:DescribeSecret" ],
8        "Resource": "arn:aws:secretsmanager:<region>:<account_id>:secret:TestEnv/*"
9      },
10     {
11       "Sid" : "Stmt2GetSecretValue",
12       "Effect": "Allow",
13       "Action": [ "secretsmanager:GetSecretValue" ],
14       "Resource": "arn:aws:secretsmanager:<region>:<account_id>:secret:TestEnv/-*",
15       "Condition" : {
16         "ForAnyValue:StringLike" : {
17           "secretsmanager:Label" : "AWSCURRENT"
18         }
19       }
20     }
```

```
21    ]
22  }
```

Because a secret version can have multiple staging labels attached, you need to use the IAM policy language's "set operators" to compare them. In the previous example, `ForAnyValue:StringLike` says that if any one of the staging labels attached to the secret version being evaluated matches the string "AWSCURRENT", then the statement matches and the `Effect` (`Allow`) is applied.

For more example identity-based policies, see Using Identity-Based Policies (IAM Policies) for AWS Secrets Manager. For more information about users, groups, roles, and permissions, see Identities (Users, Groups, and Roles) in the *IAM User Guide.*

# Using Identity-Based Policies (IAM Policies) for AWS Secrets Manager

As an administrator of an account, you can control access to the AWS resources in the account by attaching permissions policies to IAM identities (users, groups, and roles). When granting permissions, you decide who is getting the permissions, the resources they get permissions to, and the specific actions that you want to allow on those resources. If the permissions are granted to a role, that role can be assumed by users in other accounts that you specify.

By default, a user (or role) has no permissions of any kind. All permissions must be explicitly granted by a policy. If a permission is not explicitly granted, then it is implicitly denied. If a permission is explicitly denied, then that overrules any other policy that might have allowed it. In other words, a user has only those permissions that are explicitly granted and that are not explicitly denied.

For an overview of the basic elements for policies, see Managing Access to Resources with Policies.

**Topics**

- Available AWS Managed Policies for Secrets Manager
- Granting Full Secrets Manager Administrator Permissions to a User
- For the Consuming Application: Granting Read Access to One Secret
- Limiting Access to Specific Actions
- Limiting Access to Specific Secrets
- Limiting Access to Secrets that Have Specific Staging Labels or Tags
- Granting a Rotation Function Permission to Access a Separate Master Secret

## Available AWS Managed Policies for Secrets Manager

AWS Secrets Manager provides the following AWS managed policy to make granting permissions easier. Choose the link to view it in the IAM console.

- SecretsManagerReadWrite — This policy grants the access required to administer Secrets Manager, except that it does not include the IAM permissions required to create roles and attach policies to those roles. For those permissions, attach the IAMFullAccess managed policy. For instructions, see the following section Granting Full Secrets Manager Administrator Permissions to a User.

## Granting Full Secrets Manager Administrator Permissions to a User

To be a AWS Secrets Manager administrator, you must have permissions in several services. We recommended that you do not enable Secrets Manager as an end-user service that enables your users to create and manage their own secrets. The permissions required to enable rotation grant significant permissions that standard users should not have. Instead, Secrets Manager is intended to be a service managed by trusted administrators. The intended gain is that the end user no longer needs to handle the credentials directly or embed them in code.

**Warning**
When you enable rotation, Secrets Manager creates a Lambda function and an IAM role that it attaches to the function. This requires several IAM permissions that should be granted only to trusted individuals. Therefore, the managed policy for Secrets Manager purposefully *does not* include these IAM permissions. Instead, you must explicitly choose to assign the IAMFullAccess managed policy, in addition to the SecretsManagerReadWrite managed policy to create a full Secrets Manager administrator.
Granting access with only the SecretsManagerReadWrite policy enables an IAM user to create and manage secrets, but that user cannot create and configure the Lambda rotation functions required to enable rotation.

Complete the following steps to grant full AWS Secrets Manager administrator permissions to an IAM user, group, or role in your account. In this example, you don't create a new policy; instead you attach an AWS managed policy that is preconfigured with the permissions.

**To grant full admin permissions to an IAM user, group, or role**

1. Sign in to the Identity and Access Management (IAM) console at https://console.aws.amazon.com/iam/ as a user who has permissions to attach IAM policies to other IAM users.

   In the IAM console, navigate to **Policies**.

2. For **Filter: Policy type**, choose **AWS managed**, and then in the **Search** box start typing **AWSSecretsManagerFullAccess** until you can see the policy in the list.

3. Choose the **SecretsManagerReadWrite** policy name.

4. Choose the **Attached entities** tab, and then choose **Attach**.

5. Check the box next to the users, groups, or roles that you want to make a Secrets Manager administrator.

6. Choose **Attach policy**.

7. Repeat steps 1 through 6 to also attach the **IAMFullAccess** policy.

The selected users, groups, and roles can immediately begin performing tasks in Secrets Manager.

## For the Consuming Application: Granting Read Access to One Secret

When you write an application to use Secrets Manager to retrieve and use a secret, you only need to grant that application a very limited set of permissions - the action that allows retrieval of the encrypted secret value with the credentials, and the ARN of the secret

```
1  {
2      "Version": "2012-10-17",
3      "Statement": {
4          "Effect": "Allow",
5          "Action": "secretsmanager:GetSecretValue",
6          "Resource": "ARN-OF-SECRET-THE-APP-NEEDS-TO-ACCESS"
7      }
8  }
```

For a list of all the permissions that are available to assign in an IAM policy, see Actions, Resources, and Context Keys You Can Use in an IAM Policy for AWS Secrets Manager.

## Limiting Access to Specific Actions

If you want to grant limited permissions instead of full permissions, you can create a policy that lists individual permissions that you want to allow in the `Action` element of the IAM permissions policy. As shown in the following example, you can use wildcard (*) characters to grant only the `Describe*`, `Get*`, and `List*` permissions, essentially providing read-only access your secrets:

```
1  {
2      "Version": "2012-10-17",
3      "Statement": {
4          "Effect": "Allow",
5          "Action": [
6              "secretsmanager:Describe*",
7              "secretsmanager:Get*",
8              "secretsmanager:List*"
```

```
9          ],
10          "Resource": "*"
11      }
12  }
```

For a list of all the permissions that are available to assign in an IAM policy, see Actions, Resources, and Context Keys You Can Use in an IAM Policy for AWS Secrets Manager.

## Limiting Access to Specific Secrets

In addition to restricting access to specific actions, you also can restrict access to specific secrets in your account. The `Resource` elements in the previous examples all specify the wildcard character ("*"), which means "any resource that this action can interact with". Instead, you can replace the "*" with the Amazon Resource Name (ARN) of specific secrets to which you want to allow access.

### Example Example: Granting permissions to a single secret by name

The first statement of the following policy grants the user read access to the metadata about all of the secrets in the account, but the second statement allows the user to perform any Secrets Manager actions on only a single, specified secret by name, or on any secret that begins with the string "another_secret_name-" followed by exactly 6 characters:

```
1  {
2      "Version": "2012-10-17",
3      "Statement": [
4          {
5              "Effect": "Allow",
6              "Action": [
7                  "secretsmanager:DescribeSecret",
8                  "secretsmanager:List*"
9              ],
10             "Resource": "*"
11         },
12         {
13             "Effect": "Allow",
14             "Action": "secretsmanager:*",
15             "Resource": [
16                 "arn:aws:secretsmanager:<region>:<account-id-number>:secret:
                       a_specific_secret_name-a1b2c3",
17                 "arn:aws:secretsmanager:<region>:<account-id-number>:secret:another_secret_name
                       -??????"
18             ]
19         }
20     ]
21 }
```

Using the '??????' as a wildcard to match the 6 random characters assigned by Secrets Manager avoids a problem that occurs if you use the '*' wildcard instead. If you use the syntax "another_secret_name-*", it matches not just the intended secret with the 6 random characters, but it also matches "another_secret_name-<anything-here>a1b2c3". Using the '??????' syntax enables you to securely grant permissions to a secret that does not yet exist, because you can predict all of the parts of the ARN except those 6 random characters. Be aware, however, that if you delete the secret and recreate it with the same name, the user automatically receives permission to the new secret even though the 6 characters will be different.

You get the ARN for the secret from the AWS Secrets Manager console (on the **Details** page for a secret) or by calling the `List*` APIs. The user or group that you apply this policy to can perform any action (" `secretsmanager:*`") on only the two secrets identified by the Amazon Resource Name (ARN) in the example.

If you don't care about the region or account that owns a secret, you must specify a wildcard character * and not an empty field for the region and account ID number fields of the ARN.

For more information about the ARNs for various resources, see Resources That You Can Reference in an IAM Policy .

## Limiting Access to Secrets that Have Specific Staging Labels or Tags

In any of the previous examples, you called out actions, resources, and principals explicitly by name or ARN only. You can also refine access to include only those secrets that have metadata with a certain tag key and value, or a secret that has a specific label.

**Example: Granting permission to a secret with metadata that has a certain tag key and value**
The following policy, when attached to a user, group, or role, allows the user to run `GetSecret` on any secret in the current account whose metadata contains a tag with the key "ServerName" and the value "ServerABC".

```
1  {
2      "Policy": {
3          "Version": "2012-10-17",
4          "Statement": [
5              {
6                  "Effect": "Allow",
7                  "Action": "secretsmanager:DescribeSecret",
8                  "Resource": "*",
9                  "Condition": { "StringEquals": { "secretsmanager:ResourceTag/ServerName": "
                        ServerABC" } }
10             }
11         ]
12     }
13 }
```

**Example: Granting permission to the version of the secret that has a certain staging label**
The following policy, when attached to a user, group, or role, allows the user to run `GetSecret` on any secret with a name that begins with `Prod`, and only for the version that is has the staging label `AWSCURRENT` attached.

```
1  {
2      "Policy": {
3          "Version": "2012-10-17",
4          "Statement": [
5              {
6                  "Effect": "Allow",
7                  "Action": "secretsmanager:GetSecret",
8                  "Resource": "arn:aws:secretsmanager:::secret/Prod*",
9                  "Condition": { "ForAnyValue:StringEquals": { "secretsmanager:VersionStage": "
                        AWSCURRENT" } }
10             }
11         ]
12     }
13 }
```

Because a version of a secret can have multiple staging labels attached, you need to use the IAM policy language's set operators to compare them. In the previous example, `ForAnyValue:StringLike` says that if any one of the staging labels attached to the version being evaluated matches the string `AWSCURRENT`, then the statement matches and the `Effect` is applied.

## Granting a Rotation Function Permission to Access a Separate Master Secret

When you create a Lambda rotation function using the provided AWS Serverless Application Repository template, either by using the console or by using AWS CLI commands, there is a default policy attached to function's role that controls what the function can do. By default, this policy grants access *only* to secrets that have this Lambda function configured to be the secret's rotation function.

If credentials in the secret do not have permission to change their own password on the secured database or service, then you need to use a separate set of credentials with elevated permissions (a *superuser*) that can change this secret's credentials during rotation. These superuser credentials are stored in a separate "master" secret. Then, when you rotate your secret, the Lambda rotation function signs in to the database or service with the master credentials to change or update the secret's credentials. If you choose to implement this strategy, then you must add an additional statement to the role policy attached to the function that grants access to this master secret in addition to the main secret.

If you use the console to configure a rotation with a strategy that uses a master secret then you can select the master secret when you configure rotation for the secret.

**Important**
You must have **GetSecretValue** permission for the master secret to select it in the console.

After you complete configuring rotation in the console, you must manually perform the following steps to grant the Lambda function access to the master secret.

**To grant a Lambda rotation function access to a master secret**
Follow the steps in one of the following tabs:

---

[ **Using the console** ]

1. When you complete the creation of a secret with rotation enabled, or your edit your secret to enable rotation, the console displays a message similar to the following:

```
1 Your secret MyNewSecret has been successfully stored [and secret rotation is enabled].
2 To finish configuring rotation, you need to grant the role MyLambdaFunctionRole permission
    to retrieve the secret <ARN of master secret>.
```

2. Copy the ARN of the master secret in the message to your clipboard. You will paste it in a later step.

3. The role name in the preceding message is a link to the IAM console and navigates directly to that role for you. Choose that link.

4. On the **Permissions** tab, there can be one or two inline policies. One is named `SecretsManager<Name of Template>0`, and contains the EC2 related permissions required when both the rotation function and your secured service are running in a VPC and not directly accessible from the Internet. The other is named `SecretsManager<Name of Template>1` and contains the permissions that enable the rotation function to call Secrets Manager operations. Open that policy (the ending with "1") by choosing the expand arrow to the left of the policy and examining its permissions.

5. Choose **Edit policy**, and then perform the steps in one of the following tabs:

---

[ **Using the IAM Visual Editor** ]

On the **Visual editor** tab, choose **Add additional permissions**, and then set the following values:

- For **Service**, choose **Secrets Manager**.
- For **Actions**, choose **GetSecretValue**.

- For **Resources**, choose **Add ARN** next to the **secret** resource type entry.
- In the **Add ARN(s)** dialog box, paste the ARN of the master secret that you copied previously.

---

**[ Using the JSON editor ]**

On the **JSON** tab, examine the top of the script. Between lines 3 (`"Statement": [`) and line 4 ( `{` ), enter the following lines:

```
1        {
2            "Action": "secretsmanager:GetSecretValue",
3            "Resource": "arn:aws:secretsmanager:region:123456789012:secret:
                 MyDatabaseMasterSecret",
4            "Effect": "Allow"
5        },
```

---

1. When you're done editing the policy, choose **Review policy**, and then **Save changes**.

2. You can now close the IAM console and return to the AWS Secrets Manager console.

---

# Determining Access to a Secret

To determine the full extent of who or what currently has access to a secret in AWS Secrets Manager, you must examine all AWS Identity and Access Management (IAM) policies that are attached to either the IAM user and its groups or the IAM role. You might do this to determine the scope of potential usage of a secret, or to help you meet compliance or auditing requirements. The following topics can help you generate a complete list of the AWS principals (identities) that currently have access to a secret.

**Topics**

- Understanding Policy Evaluation
- Examining IAM Policies

## Understanding Policy Evaluation

When authorizing access to a secret, Secrets Manager evaluates all IAM policies attached to the IAM user or role making the request. In many cases, Secrets Manager must evaluate the IAM policies together to determine whether access to the secret is allowed or denied. To do this, Secrets Manager uses a process similar to the one described at Determining Whether a Request is Allowed or Denied in the *IAM User Guide*.

For example, assume that you have two secrets and three users, all in the same AWS account. The secrets and users have the following policies:

- Ana has no IAM policy that references Secret 1 or Secret 2.
- Bob's IAM policy allows all Secrets Manager actions for all secrets.
- Carlos' IAM policy denies all Secrets Manager actions for all secrets.

Ana cannot access either secret because there is no policy that explicitly allow her access.

Bob can access both Secret 1 and Secret 2 because Bob has an IAM policy that allows access to all secrets in the account and there is no explicit deny anywhere to override that.

Carlos cannot access Secret 1 or Secret 2 because all Secrets Manager actions are denied in his IAM policy. The explicit deny in Carlos' IAM policy overrides any explicit allow found in any other policy.

In summary, all policy statements from the identity that "allow" access are added together. Any explicit deny overrides any allow to the overlapping action and resource.

## Examining IAM Policies

To determine which identities currently have access to a secret through IAM policies, you can use the browser-based IAM Policy Simulator tool, or you can make requests to the IAM policy simulator API.

**Topics**

- Examining IAM Policies with the IAM Policy Simulator
- Examining IAM Policies with the IAM API

### Examining IAM Policies with the IAM Policy Simulator

The IAM Policy Simulator can help you learn which principals have access to a secret through an IAM policy.

**To use the IAM Policy Simulator to determine access to a KMS secret**

1. Sign in to the AWS Management Console and then open the IAM Policy Simulator at https://policysim. aws.amazon.com/.

2. In the **Users, Groups, and Roles** pane, choose the user, group, or role whose policies you want to simulate.

3. (Optional) Clear the check box next to any policies that you want to omit from the simulation. To simulate all policies, leave all policies selected.

4. In the **Policy Simulator** pane, do the following:

   1. For **Select service**, choose **AWS Secrets Manager**.

   2. To simulate specific Secrets Manager actions, for **Select actions**, choose the actions to simulate. To simulate all Secrets Manager actions, choose **Select All**.

5. (Optional) The Policy Simulator simulates access to all secrets by default. To simulate access to a specific secret, select **Simulation Settings** and then type the Amazon Resource Name (ARN) of the secret to simulate.

6. Select **Run Simulation**.

You can view the results of the simulation in the **Results** section. Repeat steps 2 through 6 for every IAM user, group, and role in the AWS account.

## Examining IAM Policies with the IAM API

You can use the IAM API to examine IAM policies programmatically. The following steps provide a general overview of how to do this:

1. For each AWS account listed as a principal in the secret's policy (that is, each *root account* listed in this format: `"Principal": {"AWS": "arn:aws:iam::accountnumber:root"}`), use the ListUsers and ListRoles operations in the IAM API to retrieve a list of every IAM user and role in that account.

2. For each IAM user and role in the list, use the SimulatePrincipalPolicy operation in the IAM API, passing in the following parameters:

   - For `PolicySourceArn`, specify the Amazon Resource Name (ARN) of a user or role from your list. You can specify only one `PolicySourceArn` for each `SimulatePrincipalPolicy` API request, so you must call this API multiple times, once for each IAM user and role in your list.
   - For the `ActionNames` list, specify every AWS Secrets Manager API action to simulate. To simulate all Secrets Manager API actions, use `secretsmanager:*`. To test individual Secrets Manager API actions, precede each API action with "secretsmanager:", for example "secretsmanager:ListSecrets". For a complete list of all Secrets Manager API actions, see Actions in the *AWS Key Management Service API Reference*.
   - (Optional) To determine whether the IAM users or roles have access to specific secrets, use the `ResourceArns` parameter to specify a list of the Amazon Resource Names (ARNs) of the secrets. To determine whether the IAM users or roles have access to any secret, do not use the `ResourceArns` parameter.

IAM responds to each `SimulatePrincipalPolicy` API request with an evaluation decision: `allowed`, `explicitDeny`, or `implicitDeny`. For each response that contains an evaluation decision of `allowed`, the response will also contain the name of the specific Secrets Manager API action that is allowed and, if applicable, the ARN of the secret that was used in the evaluation.

# Monitor the Use of Your AWS Secrets Manager Secrets

As a best practice, you should monitor your secrets to make sure that usage of your secrets and any changes to them are logged. This helps you to ensure that any unexpected usage or change can be investigated, and unwanted changes can be rolled back. AWS Secrets Manager currently supports two AWS services that enable you to monitor your organization and the activity that happens within it.

**Topics**

- AWS CloudTrail
- Amazon CloudWatch Events

## AWS CloudTrail

AWS Secrets Manager is integrated with AWS CloudTrail (a service that captures AWS Secrets Manager API calls), and delivers the log files to an Amazon S3 bucket that you specify. CloudTrail can capture all API calls that are generated by either the Secrets Manager console or your code. By using the information that CloudTrail collects, you can determine various things—the secret access request that was made to Secrets Manager, the source IP address from which the request was made, who made the request, when it was made, and so on. Secrets Manager is also integrated with the **Event history** feature in CloudTrail. If an API for Secrets Manager is supported in **Event history**, you can view the most recent 90 days of events in Secrets Manager. You can view this in the CloudTrail console in **Event history**. You can do this even if you haven't configured any logs in CloudTrail.

To learn more about CloudTrail, including how to configure and enable it, see the AWS CloudTrail User Guide.

### Secrets Manager Information in CloudTrail

CloudTrail is enabled on your AWS account when you create the account. When activity occurs in Secrets Manager, that activity is recorded in a CloudTrail event, and in other AWS service events in **Event history**. You can view, search, and download the past 90 days of supported activity in your AWS account. For more information, see Viewing Events with CloudTrail Event History and Services Supported by CloudTrail Event History.

When CloudTrail logging is enabled in your AWS account, API calls made to Secrets Manager operations are tracked in CloudTrail log files, where they are written with other AWS service records. CloudTrail determines when to create and write to a new file based on a time period and file size.

Secrets Manager currently supports logging only the following operations as management events in CloudTrail log files. There are currently no data events.

- CancelRotateSecret
- CreateSecret
- DeleteSecret
- GetSecretValue
- PutSecretValue
- RestoreSecret
- RotateSecret
- TagResource
- UntagResource
- UpdateSecret
- UpdateSecretVersionStage

Every log entry contains information about who generated the request. The user-identity information in the log entry helps you determine the following:

- Whether the request was made with account root or IAM user credentials
- Whether the request was made with temporary security credentials for an IAM role or a federated user whose security credentials are validated by an external identity provider (IdP) instead of directly by AWS
- Whether the request was made by another AWS service

For more information, see the CloudTrail userIdentity Element.

You can view, search, and download the most recent 90 days of AWS Secrets Manager activity in the CloudTrail console. For more information, see Viewing Events with CloudTrail Event History. You can also create a trail and store your log files in your Amazon S3 bucket for as long as you want. You can define Amazon S3 lifecycle rules to automatically archive or delete log files. By default, your log files are encrypted with Amazon S3 server-side encryption (SSE).

If you want to be notified when log files are delivered, you can configure CloudTrail to publish Amazon SNS notifications whenever new log files are delivered. For more information, see Configuring Amazon SNS Notifications for CloudTrail.

You also can aggregate AWS Secrets Manager log files from multiple AWS Regions and multiple AWS accounts into a single Amazon S3 bucket.

For more information, see Receiving CloudTrail Log Files from Multiple Regions and Receiving CloudTrail Log Files from Multiple Accounts.

**Retrieving Secrets Manager Log File Entries**

You can retrieve individual events from CloudTrail by using any of the following techniques:

**To retrieve Secrets Manager events from CloudTrail logs**

---

[ **Using the AWS Management Console** ]

The CloudTrail console enables you to view events that occurred within the past 90 days.

1. Open the CloudTrail console at https://console.aws.amazon.com/cloudtrail/.

2. Ensure that the console is pointing at the region where your events occurred. The console shows only those events that occurred in the selected region. Choose the region from the drop-down list in the upper-right corner of the console.

3. In the left-hand navigation pane, choose **Event history**.

4. Choose **Filter** criteria and/or a **Time range** to help you find the event that you're looking for. For example, to see all Secrets Manager events, for **Select attribute**, choose **Event source**. Then, for **Enter event source**, choose **secretsmanager.amazonaws.com**.

5. To see additional details, choose the expand arrow next to event you want to view. To see all of the information available, choose **View event**.

---

[ **Using the AWS CLI or SDK Operations** ]

1. Open a command window where you can run AWS CLI commands.

2. Run a command similar to the following example. The output is shown as word wrapped here for readability, but the real output isn't.

```
1  $ aws cloudtrail lookup-events --region us-east-1 --lookup-attributes AttributeKey=
     EventSource,AttributeValue=secretsmanager.amazonaws.com
2  {
3      "Events": [
4          {
5              "EventId": "EXAMPLE1-90ab-cdef-fedc-ba987EXAMPLE",
6              "EventName": "CreateSecret",
7              "EventTime": 1525106994.0,
8              "Username": "Administrator",
9              "Resources": [],
10             "CloudTrailEvent": "{\"eventVersion\":\"1.05\",\"userIdentity\":{\"type\":\"
                 IAMUser\",\"principalId\":\"AKIAIOSFODNN7EXAMPLE\",
11                 \"arn\":\"arn:aws:iam::123456789012:user/Administrator\",\"accountId
                     \":\"123456789012\",\"accessKeyId\":\"AKIAIOSFODNN7EXAMPLE\",
12                 \"userName\":\"Administrator\"},\"eventTime\":\"2018-04-30T16:49:54Z\",\"
                     eventSource\":\"secretsmanager.amazonaws.com\",
13                 \"eventName\":\"CreateSecret\",\"awsRegion\":\"us-east-1\",\"
                     sourceIPAddress\":\"192.168.100.101\",
14                 \"userAgent\":\"<useragent string>\",\"requestParameters\":{\"name\":\"
                     MyTestSecret\",
15                 \"clientRequestToken\":\"EXAMPLE2-90ab-cdef-fedc-ba987EXAMPLE\"},\"
                     responseElements\":null,
16                 \"requestID\":\"EXAMPLE3-90ab-cdef-fedc-ba987EXAMPLE\",\"eventID\":\"
                     EXAMPLE4-90ab-cdef-fedc-ba987EXAMPLE\",
17                 \"eventType\":\"AwsApiCall\",\"recipientAccountId\":\"123456789012\"}"
18         }
19     ]
20 }
```

**Understanding Secrets Manager Log File Entries**

CloudTrail log files can contain one or more log entries. Each entry lists multiple JSON-formatted events. A log entry represents a single request from any source and includes information about the requested operation, the date and time of the operation, request parameters, and so on. Log entries aren't an ordered stack trace of the public API calls, so they don't appear in any specific order.

The following example shows a CloudTrail log entry for a sample `CreateSecret` call:

```
1  {
2    "eventVersion": "1.05",
3    "userIdentity": {
4      "type": "Root",
5      "principalId": "123456789012",
6      "arn": "arn:aws:iam::123456789012:root",
7      "accountId": "123456789012",
8      "accessKeyId": "AKIAIOSFODNN7EXAMPLE",
9      "userName": "myusername",
10     "sessionContext": {"attributes": {
11       "mfaAuthenticated": "false",
12       "creationDate": "2018-04-03T17:43:50Z"
13     }}
14   },
15   "eventTime": "2018-04-03T17:50:55Z",
```

```
16      "eventSource": "secretsmanager.amazonaws.com",
17      "eventName": "CreateSecret",
18      "awsRegion": "us-west-2",
19      "requestParameters": {
20        "name": "MyDatabaseSecret",
21        "clientRequestToken": "EXAMPLE1-90ab-cdef-fedc-ba987EXAMPLE"
22      },
23      "responseElements": null,
24      "requestID": "EXAMPLE2-90ab-cdef-fedc-ba987EXAMPLE",
25      "eventID": "EXAMPLE3-90ab-cdef-fedc-ba987EXAMPLE",
26      "eventType": "AwsApiCall",
27      "recipientAccountId": "123456789012"
28 }
```

The following example shows a CloudTrail log entry for a sample DeleteSecret call:

```
1  {
2      "eventVersion": "1.05",
3      "userIdentity": {
4        "type": "Root",
5        "principalId": "123456789012",
6        "arn": "arn:aws:iam::123456789012:root",
7        "accountId": "123456789012",
8        "accessKeyId": "AKIAIOSFODNN7EXAMPLE",
9        "userName": "myusername",
10       "sessionContext": {"attributes": {
11         "mfaAuthenticated": "false",
12         "creationDate": "2018-04-03T17:43:50Z"
13       }}
14     },
15     "eventTime": "2018-04-03T17:51:02Z",
16     "eventSource": "secretsmanager.amazonaws.com",
17     "eventName": "DeleteSecret",
18     "awsRegion": "us-west-2",
19     "requestParameters": {
20       "recoveryWindowInDays": 30,
21       "secretId": "MyDatabaseSecret"
22     },
23     "responseElements": {
24       "name": "MyDatabaseSecret",
25       "deletionDate": "May 3, 2018 5:51:02 PM",
26       "aRN": "arn:aws:secretsmanager:us-west-2:123456789012:secret:MyDatabaseSecret-a1b2c3"
27     },
28     "requestID": "EXAMPLE2-90ab-cdef-fedc-ba987EXAMPLE",
29     "eventID": "EXAMPLE3-90ab-cdef-fedc-ba987EXAMPLE",
30     "eventType": "AwsApiCall",
31     "recipientAccountId": "123456789012"
32 }
```

## Amazon CloudWatch Events

Secrets Manager can work with CloudWatch Events to trigger alerts when administrator-specified operations occur in an organization. For example, because of the sensitivity of such operations, administrators might want to be warned when a secret is deleted or when a secret is rotated. Another common need is for an alert if anyone tries to use a secret version while it's in its waiting period to be deleted. You can configure CloudWatch Events rules that look for these operations and then send the generated events to administrator defined "targets". A target could be an Amazon SNS topic that emails or text messages its subscribers. You can also create a simple AWS Lambda function that's triggered by the event, which logs the details of the operation for your later review.

To learn more about CloudWatch Events, including how to configure and enable it, see the Amazon CloudWatch Events User Guide.

### Monitoring Secret Versions Scheduled for Deletion

You can use a combination of AWS CloudTrail, Amazon CloudWatch Logs, and Amazon Simple Notification Service (Amazon SNS) to create an alarm that notifies you of any attempts to access a version of a secret that's pending deletion. If you receive a notification from such an alarm, you might want to cancel deletion of the secret to give yourself more time to determine whether you really want to delete it. Your investigation might result in the secret being restored because it really is still needed. Alternatively, you might need to update the user with details of the new secret that they really should be using.

The following procedures explain how to receive a notification when a request for the `GetSecretValue` operation that results in a specific error message is written to your CloudTrail log files. Other API operations can be performed on the version of the secret without triggering the alarm. The intent of this CloudWatch alarm is to detect usage that might indicate that a person or application is still trying to use credentials that should no longer be used.

Before you begin these procedures, you must have already turned on CloudTrail in the AWS Region and account where you intend to monitor AWS Secrets ManagerAPI requests. For instructions, go to Creating a Trail for the First Time in the *AWS CloudTrail User Guide*.

### Topics

- Part 1: Configure CloudTrail Log File Delivery to CloudWatch Logs
- Part 2: Create the CloudWatch Alarm
-

### Part 1: Configure CloudTrail Log File Delivery to CloudWatch Logs

You must configure delivery of your CloudTrail log files to CloudWatch Logs. You do this so that CloudWatch Logs can monitor them for Secrets Manager API requests to retrieve a version of a secret that's pending deletion.

### To configure CloudTrail log file delivery to CloudWatch Logs

1. Open the CloudTrail console at https://console.aws.amazon.com/cloudtrail/.

2. On the top navigation bar, choose the AWS Region where you want to monitor secrets.

3. In the left navigation pane, choose **Trails**, and then choose the name of the trail you want to configure for CloudWatch.

4. On the **Trails Configuration** page, scroll down to the **CloudWatch Logs** section, and then choose the edit icon (✎).

5. For **New or existing log group**, type a name for the log group, such as **CloudTrail/MyCloud-WatchLogGroup**.

6. For **IAM role**, you can use the default role named **CloudTrail_CloudWatchLogs_Role**. That role has a default role policy with the required permissions to deliver CloudTrail events to the log group.

7. Choose **Continue** to save your configuration.

8. On the **AWS CloudTrail will deliver CloudTrail events associated with API activity in your account to your CloudWatch Logs log group** page, choose **Allow**.

## Part 2: Create the CloudWatch Alarm

To receive a notification when a Secrets Manager `GetSecretValue` API operation requests to access a version of a secret that's pending deletion, you must create a CloudWatch alarm and configure notification.

### To create a CloudWatch alarm that monitors usage of a version of a secret that's pending deletion

1. Sign in to the CloudWatch console at https://console.aws.amazon.com/cloudwatch/.

2. On the top navigation bar, choose the AWS Region where you want to monitor secrets.

3. In the left navigation pane, choose **Logs**.

4. In the list of **Log Groups**, select the check box next to the log group that you created in the previous procedure, such as **CloudTrail/MyCloudWatchLogGroup**. Then choose **Create Metric Filter**.

5. For **Filter Pattern**, type or paste the following:

```
1 { $.eventName = "GetSecretValue" && $.errorMessage = "*secret because it was deleted*" }
```

   Choose **Assign Metric**.

6. On the **Create Metric Filter and Assign a Metric** page, do the following:

   1. For **Metric Namespace**, type **CloudTrailLogMetrics**.

   2. For **Metric Name**, type **AttemptsToAccessDeletedSecrets**.

   3. Choose **Show advanced metric settings**, and then if necessary for **Metric Value**, type **1**.

   4. Choose **Create Filter**.

7. In the filter box, choose **Create Alarm**.

8. In the **Create Alarm** window, do the following:

   1. For **Name**, type **AttemptsToAccessDeletedSecretsAlarm**.

   2. **Whenever:**, for **is:**, choose **>=**, and then type **1**.

   3. Next to **Send notification to:**, do one of the following:

      - To create and use a new Amazon SNS topic, choose **New list**, and then type a new topic name. For **Email list:**, type at least one email address. You can type more than one email address by separating them with commas.
      - To use an existing Amazon SNS topic, choose the name of the topic to use. If a list isn't available, choose **Select list**.

   4. Choose **Create Alarm**.

Your alarm is now in place. To test it, create a version of a secret and then schedule it for deletion. Then, try to retrieve the secret value. You'll shortly receive an email at the address that's configured in the alarm. It will alert you to the use of a secret version that's scheduled for deletion.

# AWS Secrets Manager Reference

Use the topics in this section to find detailed reference information for various aspects of AWS Secrets Manager.

**Topics**

- Limits of AWS Secrets Manager
- AWS Templates You Can Use to Create Lambda Rotation Functions
- AWS Managed Policies Available for Use with AWS Secrets Manager
- Actions, Resources, and Context Keys You Can Use in an IAM Policy for AWS Secrets Manager

# Limits of AWS Secrets Manager

This section specifies limits that affect AWS Secrets Manager.

## Limits on Names

The following are restrictions on names that you create in AWS Secrets Manager (including names of secrets):

- They must be composed of Unicode characters.
- They must not exceed 256 characters in length.

## Maximum and Minimum Values

The following are the default maximums for entities in AWS Secrets Manager:

| | |
|---|---|
| Max number of secrets in an AWS account | 40,000 |
| Max number of versions in a secret | ~100 |
| Max number of labels you can attach to a version | 20 |
| Max number of versions a label can be attached to at the same time | 1 |
| Maximum length of a secret | 4096 characters |

# AWS Templates You Can Use to Create Lambda Rotation Functions

This section identifies the AWS managed templates that you can use to create a Lambda rotation function for your AWS Secrets Manager secret. These templates are associated with the AWS Serverless Application Repository, which uses AWS CloudFormation to create 'stacks' of preconfigured resources. In this case, they create a stack that consists of the Lambda function and an IAM role that Secrets Manager can assume to invoke the function when rotation occurs.

**To create a Lambda rotation function with any of the following templates, you can copy and paste the ARN of the specified template into the CLI commands described in the topic Rotating AWS Secrets Manager Secrets for Other Databases or Services.**

Each of the following templates creates a Lambda rotation function for a different combination of database and rotation strategy. The first bullet under each shows the database or service that the function supports. The second bullet describes the rotation strategy that's implemented by the function. The third bullet specifies the JSON structure that the rotation function expects to find in the `SecretString` value of the secret being rotated.

## RDS MySQL Single User

```
1 arn:aws:serverlessrepo:us-east-1:297356227824:applications/
     SecretsManagerRDSMySQLRotationSingleUser
```

- **Name:** SecretsManagerRDSMySQLRotationSingleUser

- **Supported database/service:** MySQL database that's hosted on an Amazon Relational Database Service (Amazon RDS) database instance.

- **Rotation strategy:** This changes the password for a user whose credentials are stored in the secret that's rotated. For more information about this strategy, see Rotating AWS Secrets Manager Secrets for One User with a Single Password.

- **Expected `SecretString` structure:**

```
1 {
2   "engine": "mysql",
3   "host": "<required: instance host name/resolvable DNS name>",
4   "username": "<required: username>",
5   "password": "<required: password>",
6   "dbname": "<optional: database name. If not specified, defaults to None>",
7   "port": "<optional: TCP port number. If not specified, defaults to 3306>"
8 }
```

- **Source code:** Secrets Manager Lambda Rotation Template: RDS MySQL Single User

## RDS MySQL Master User

```
1 arn:aws:serverlessrepo:us-east-1:297356227824:applications/
     SecretsManagerRDSMySQLRotationMultiUser
```

- **Name:** SecretsManagerRDSMySQLRotationMultiUser

- **Supported database/service:** MySQL database that's hosted on an Amazon RDS database instance.

- **Rotation strategy:** Two users are alternated during rotation by using the credentials of a separate master user, which is stored in a separate secret. The user that's not currently active has its password changed before it's made the active user. For more information about this strategy, see Rotating AWS Secrets Manager Secrets by Alternating Between Two Existing Users.

- Expected `SecretString` structure:

```
1 {
2    "engine": "mysql",
3    "host": "<required: instance host name/resolvable DNS name>",
4    "username": "<required: username>",
5    "password": "<required: password>",
6    "dbname": "<optional: database name. If not specified, defaults to None>",
7    "port": "<optional: TCP port number. If not specified, defaults to 3306>",
8    "masterarn": "<required: the ARN of the master secret used to create 2nd user and change
         passwords>"
9 }
```

- **Source code:** Secrets Manager Lambda Rotation Template: RDS MySQL Multiple User

# RDS PostgreSQL Single User

```
1 arn:aws:serverlessrepo:us-east-1:297356227824:applications/
     SecretsManagerRDSPostgreSQLRotationSingleUser
```

- **Name:** SecretsManagerRDSPostgreSQLRotationSingleUser

- **Supported database/service:** PostgreSQL database that's hosted on an Amazon RDS database instance.

- **Rotation strategy:** This changes the password for a user whose credentials are stored in the secret that's rotated. For more information about this strategy, see Rotating AWS Secrets Manager Secrets for One User with a Single Password.

- Expected `SecretString` structure:

```
1 {
2    "engine": "postgres",
3    "host": "<required: instance host name/resolvable DNS name>",
4    "username": "<required: username>",
5    "password": "<required: password>",
6    "dbname": "<optional: database name. If not specified, defaults to 'postgres'>",
7    "port": "<optional: TCP port number. If not specified, defaults to 5432>"
8 }
```

- **Source code:** Secrets Manager Lambda Rotation Template: RDS PostgreSQL Single User

# RDS PostgreSQL Master User

```
1 arn:aws:serverlessrepo:us-east-1:297356227824:applications/
     SecretsManagerRDSPostgreSQLRotationMultiUser
```

- **Name:** SecretsManagerRDSPostgreSQLRotationMultiUser

- **Supported database/service:** PostgreSQL database that's hosted on an Amazon RDS database instance.

- **Rotation strategy:** Two users are alternated during rotation by using the credentials of a separate master user, which is stored in a separate secret. The user that's not currently active has its password changed before it's made the active user. For more information about this strategy, see Rotating AWS Secrets Manager Secrets by Alternating Between Two Existing Users.

- Expected `SecretString` structure:

```
1 {
2   "engine": "postgres",
3   "host": "<required: instance host name/resolvable DNS name>",
4   "username": "<required: username>",
5   "password": "<required: password>",
6   "dbname": "<optional: database name. If not specified, defaults to 'postgres'>",
7   "port": "<optional: TCP port number. If not specified, defaults to 5432>",
8   "masterarn": "<required: the ARN of the master secret used to create 2nd user and change
         passwords>"
9 }
```

- **Source code:** Secrets Manager Lambda Rotation Template: RDS PostgreSQL Single User

## Generic Rotation Function Template

```
1 arn:aws:serverlessrepo:us-east-1:297356227824:applications/SecretsManagerRotationTemplate
```

- **Name:** SecretsManagerRotationTemplate
- **Supported database/service:** None. You supply the code to interact with whatever service you want.
- **Rotation strategy:** None. You supply the code to implement whatever rotation strategy you want. For more information about customizing your own function, see Understanding and Customizing Your Lambda Rotation Function.
- **Expected SecretString structure:** You define this as part of the code that you write.
- **Source code:** Secrets Manager Lambda Rotation Template: Generic Template That You Must Customize and Complete

# Secrets Manager Lambda Rotation Template: Generic Template That You Must Customize and Complete

The following is the source code that's initially placed into the Lambda rotation function when you choose the **SecretsManagerRotationTemplate** template option from the AWS Serverless Application Repository. This template is never provided by choosing options in the console. Instead, to create this function manually, follow the instructions at Rotating AWS Secrets Manager Secrets for Other Databases or Services and specify this template.

For more information about creating your own rotation function, see Overview of the Lambda Rotation Function.

This template function is written in Python, and uses the AWS Boto3 SDK for Python.

```python
 1 import boto3
 2 import logging
 3 import os
 4
 5 logger = logging.getLogger()
 6 logger.setLevel(logging.INFO)
 7
 8
 9 def lambda_handler(event, context):
10     """Secrets Manager Rotation Template
11
12     This is a template for creating an AWS Secrets Manager rotation lambda
13
14     Args:
15         event (dict): Lambda dictionary of event parameters. These keys must include the
                following:
16             - SecretId: The secret ARN or identifier
17             - ClientRequestToken: The ClientRequestToken of the secret version
18             - Step: The rotation step (one of createSecret, setSecret, testSecret, or
                    finishSecret)
19
20         context (LambdaContext): The Lambda runtime information
21
22     Raises:
23         ResourceNotFoundException: If the secret with the specified arn and stage does not exist
24
25         ValueError: If the secret is not properly configured for rotation
26
27         KeyError: If the event parameters do not contain the expected keys
28
29     """
30     arn = event['SecretId']
31     token = event['ClientRequestToken']
32     step = event['Step']
33
34     # Setup the client
35     service_client = boto3.client('secretsmanager', endpoint_url=os.environ['
            SECRETS_MANAGER_ENDPOINT'])
36
37     # Make sure the version is staged correctly
38     metadata = service_client.describe_secret(SecretId=arn)
39     if not metadata['RotationEnabled']:
```

113

```
40          logger.error("Secret %s is not enabled for rotation" % arn)
41          raise ValueError("Secret %s is not enabled for rotation" % arn)
42      versions = metadata['VersionIdsToStages']
43      if token not in versions:
44          logger.error("Secret version %s has no stage for rotation of secret %s." % (token, arn))
45          raise ValueError("Secret version %s has no stage for rotation of secret %s." % (token,
                  arn))
46      if "AWSCURRENT" in versions[token]:
47          logger.info("Secret version %s already set as AWSCURRENT for secret %s." % (token, arn))
48          return
49      elif "AWSPENDING" not in versions[token]:
50          logger.error("Secret version %s not set as AWSPENDING for rotation of secret %s." % (
                  token, arn))
51          raise ValueError("Secret version %s not set as AWSPENDING for rotation of secret %s." %
                  (token, arn))
52
53      if step == "createSecret":
54          create_secret(service_client, arn, token)
55
56      elif step == "setSecret":
57          set_secret(service_client, arn, token)
58
59      elif step == "testSecret":
60          test_secret(service_client, arn, token)
61
62      elif step == "finishSecret":
63          finish_secret(service_client, arn, token)
64
65      else:
66          raise ValueError("Invalid step parameter")
67
68
69  def create_secret(service_client, arn, token):
70      """Create the secret
71
72      This method first checks for the existence of a secret for the passed in token. If one does
              not exist, it will generate a
73      new secret and put it with the passed in token.
74
75      Args:
76          service_client (client): The secrets manager service client
77
78          arn (string): The secret ARN or other identifier
79
80          token (string): The ClientRequestToken associated with the secret version
81
82      Raises:
83          ResourceNotFoundException: If the secret with the specified arn and stage does not exist
84
85      """
86      # Make sure the current secret exists
87      service_client.get_secret_value(SecretId=arn, VersionStage="AWSCURRENT")
88
89      # Now try to get the secret version, if that fails, put a new secret
```

```python
90      try:
91          service_client.get_secret_value(SecretId=arn, VersionId=token, VersionStage="AWSPENDING
                ")
92          logger.info("createSecret: Successfully retrieved secret for %s." % arn)
93      except service_client.exceptions.ResourceNotFoundException:
94          # Generate a random password
95          passwd = service_client.get_random_password(ExcludeCharacters='/@"\'\\')
96
97          # Put the secret
98          service_client.put_secret_value(SecretId=arn, ClientRequestToken=token, SecretString=
                passwd['RandomPassword'], VersionStages=['AWSPENDING'])
99          logger.info("createSecret: Successfully put secret for ARN %s and version %s." % (arn,
                token))
100
101
102 def set_secret(service_client, arn, token):
103     """Set the secret
104
105     This method should set the AWSPENDING secret in the service that the secret belongs to. For
            example, if the secret is a database
106     credential, this method should take the value of the AWSPENDING secret and set the user's
            password to this value in the database.
107
108     Args:
109         service_client (client): The secrets manager service client
110
111         arn (string): The secret ARN or other identifier
112
113         token (string): The ClientRequestToken associated with the secret version
114
115     """
116     # This is where the secret should be set in the service
117     raise NotImplementedError
118
119
120 def test_secret(service_client, arn, token):
121     """Test the secret
122
123     This method should validate that the AWSPENDING secret works in the service that the secret
            belongs to. For example, if the secret
124     is a database credential, this method should validate that the user can login with the
            password in AWSPENDING and that the user has
125     all of the expected permissions against the database.
126
127     Args:
128         service_client (client): The secrets manager service client
129
130         arn (string): The secret ARN or other identifier
131
132         token (string): The ClientRequestToken associated with the secret version
133
134     """
135     # This is where the secret should be tested against the service
136     raise NotImplementedError
```

```python
137
138
139 def finish_secret(service_client, arn, token):
140     """Finish the secret
141
142     This method finalizes the rotation process by marking the secret version passed in as the
            AWSCURRENT secret.
143
144     Args:
145         service_client (client): The secrets manager service client
146
147         arn (string): The secret ARN or other identifier
148
149         token (string): The ClientRequestToken associated with the secret version
150
151     Raises:
152         ResourceNotFoundException: If the secret with the specified arn does not exist
153
154     """
155     # First describe the secret to get the current version
156     metadata = service_client.describe_secret(SecretId=arn)
157     current_version = None
158     for version in metadata["VersionIdsToStages"]:
159         if "AWSCURRENT" in metadata["VersionIdsToStages"][version]:
160             if version == token:
161                 # The correct version is already marked as current, return
162                 logger.info("finishSecret: Version %s already marked as AWSCURRENT for %s" % (
                        version, arn))
163                 return
164             current_version = version
165             break
166
167     # Finalize by staging the secret version current
168     service_client.update_secret_version_stage(SecretId=arn, VersionStage="AWSCURRENT",
            MoveToVersionId=token, RemoveFromVersionId=current_version)
169     logger.info("finishSecret: Successfully set AWSCURRENT stage to version %s for secret %s." %
            (version, arn))
```

# Secrets Manager Lambda Rotation Template: RDS MySQL Single User

The following is the source code that's initially placed into the Lambda rotation function when you choose the **SecretsManagerRDSMySQLRotationSingleUser** template option from the AWS Serverless Application Repository. This template is automatically used to create the function when you enable rotation by using the Secrets Manager console. (In the console, you specify that the secret is for an Amazon RDS MySQL database, and that you want to rotate the secret using the credentials that are stored in the same secret.)

To create this function manually, follow the instructions at Rotating AWS Secrets Manager Secrets for Other Databases or Services, and specify this template.

For more information about the rotation strategy that's implemented by this function, see Rotating AWS Secrets Manager Secrets for One User with a Single Password.

This function is written in Python, and uses the AWS Boto3 SDK for Python.

```
1  import boto3
2  import json
3  import logging
4  import os
5  import pymysql
6
7  logger = logging.getLogger()
8  logger.setLevel(logging.INFO)
9
10
11 def lambda_handler(event, context):
12     """Secrets Manager RDS MySQL Handler
13
14     This handler uses the single-user rotation scheme to rotate an RDS MySQL user credential.
           This rotation scheme
15     logs into the database as the user and rotates the user's own password, immediately
           invalidating the user's
16     previous password.
17
18     The Secret SecretString is expected to be a JSON string with the following format:
19     {
20         'engine': <required: must be set to 'mysql'>,
21         'host': <required: instance host name>,
22         'username': <required: username>,
23         'password': <required: password>,
24         'dbname': <optional: database name>,
25         'port': <optional: if not specified, default port 3306 will be used>
26     }
27
28     Args:
29         event (dict): Lambda dictionary of event parameters. These keys must include the
               following:
30             - SecretId: The secret ARN or identifier
31             - ClientRequestToken: The ClientRequestToken of the secret version
32             - Step: The rotation step (one of createSecret, setSecret, testSecret, or
                   finishSecret)
33
34         context (LambdaContext): The Lambda runtime information
```

```
35
36      Raises:
37          ResourceNotFoundException: If the secret with the specified arn and stage does not exist
38
39          ValueError: If the secret is not properly configured for rotation
40
41          KeyError: If the secret json does not contain the expected keys
42
43      """
44      arn = event['SecretId']
45      token = event['ClientRequestToken']
46      step = event['Step']
47
48      # Setup the client
49      service_client = boto3.client('secretsmanager', endpoint_url=os.environ['
            SECRETS_MANAGER_ENDPOINT'])
50
51      # Make sure the version is staged correctly
52      metadata = service_client.describe_secret(SecretId=arn)
53      if "RotationEnabled" in metadata and not metadata['RotationEnabled']:
54          logger.error("Secret %s is not enabled for rotation" % arn)
55          raise ValueError("Secret %s is not enabled for rotation" % arn)
56      versions = metadata['VersionIdsToStages']
57      if token not in versions:
58          logger.error("Secret version %s has no stage for rotation of secret %s." % (token, arn))
59          raise ValueError("Secret version %s has no stage for rotation of secret %s." % (token,
                arn))
60      if "AWSCURRENT" in versions[token]:
61          logger.info("Secret version %s already set as AWSCURRENT for secret %s." % (token, arn))
62          return
63      elif "AWSPENDING" not in versions[token]:
64          logger.error("Secret version %s not set as AWSPENDING for rotation of secret %s." % (
                token, arn))
65          raise ValueError("Secret version %s not set as AWSPENDING for rotation of secret %s." %
                (token, arn))
66
67      # Call the appropriate step
68      if step == "createSecret":
69          create_secret(service_client, arn, token)
70
71      elif step == "setSecret":
72          set_secret(service_client, arn, token)
73
74      elif step == "testSecret":
75          test_secret(service_client, arn, token)
76
77      elif step == "finishSecret":
78          finish_secret(service_client, arn, token)
79
80      else:
81          logger.error("lambda_handler: Invalid step parameter %s for secret %s" % (step, arn))
82          raise ValueError("Invalid step parameter %s for secret %s" % (step, arn))
83
84
```

```
85 def create_secret(service_client, arn, token):
86     """Generate a new secret
87
88     This method first checks for the existence of a secret for the passed in token. If one does
           not exist, it will generate a
89     new secret and put it with the passed in token.
90
91     Args:
92         service_client (client): The secrets manager service client
93
94         arn (string): The secret ARN or other identifier
95
96         token (string): The ClientRequestToken associated with the secret version
97
98     Raises:
99         ValueError: If the current secret is not valid JSON
100
101        KeyError: If the secret json does not contain the expected keys
102
103    """
104    # Make sure the current secret exists
105    current_dict = get_secret_dict(service_client, arn, "AWSCURRENT")
106
107    # Now try to get the secret version, if that fails, put a new secret
108    try:
109        get_secret_dict(service_client, arn, "AWSPENDING", token)
110        logger.info("createSecret: Successfully retrieved secret for %s." % arn)
111    except service_client.exceptions.ResourceNotFoundException:
112        # Generate a random password
113        passwd = service_client.get_random_password(ExcludeCharacters='/@"\'\\')
114        current_dict['password'] = passwd['RandomPassword']
115
116        # Put the secret
117        service_client.put_secret_value(SecretId=arn, ClientRequestToken=token, SecretString=
               json.dumps(current_dict), VersionStages=['AWSPENDING'])
118        logger.info("createSecret: Successfully put secret for ARN %s and version %s." % (arn,
               token))
119
120
121 def set_secret(service_client, arn, token):
122     """Set the pending secret in the database
123
124     This method tries to login to the database with the AWSPENDING secret and returns on success
           . If that fails, it
125     tries to login with the AWSCURRENT and AWSPREVIOUS secrets. If either one succeeds, it sets
           the AWSPENDING password
126     as the user password in the database. Else, it throws a ValueError.
127
128     Args:
129         service_client (client): The secrets manager service client
130
131         arn (string): The secret ARN or other identifier
132
133         token (string): The ClientRequestToken associated with the secret version
```

```
134
135      Raises:
136          ResourceNotFoundException: If the secret with the specified arn and stage does not exist
137
138          ValueError: If the secret is not valid JSON or valid credentials are found to login to
                 the database
139
140          KeyError: If the secret json does not contain the expected keys
141
142      """
143      # First try to login with the pending secret, if it succeeds, return
144      pending_dict = get_secret_dict(service_client, arn, "AWSPENDING", token)
145      conn = get_connection(pending_dict)
146      if conn:
147          conn.close()
148          logger.info("setSecret: AWSPENDING secret is already set as password in MySQL DB for
                 secret arn %s." % arn)
149          return
150
151      # Now try the current password
152      conn = get_connection(get_secret_dict(service_client, arn, "AWSCURRENT"))
153      if not conn:
154          # If both current and pending do not work, try previous
155          try:
156              conn = get_connection(get_secret_dict(service_client, arn, "AWSPREVIOUS"))
157          except service_client.exceptions.ResourceNotFoundException:
158              conn = None
159
160      # If we still don't have a connection, raise a ValueError
161      if not conn:
162          logger.error("setSecret: Unable to log into database with previous, current, or pending
                 secret of secret arn %s" % arn)
163          raise ValueError("Unable to log into database with previous, current, or pending secret
                 of secret arn %s" % arn)
164
165      # Now set the password to the pending password
166      try:
167          with conn.cursor() as cur:
168              cur.execute("SET PASSWORD = PASSWORD(%s)", pending_dict['password'])
169              conn.commit()
170              logger.info("setSecret: Successfully set password for user %s in MySQL DB for secret
                     arn %s." % (pending_dict['username'], arn))
171      finally:
172          conn.close()
173
174
175  def test_secret(service_client, arn, token):
176      """Test the pending secret against the database
177
178      This method tries to log into the database with the secrets staged with AWSPENDING and runs
179      a permissions check to ensure the user has the corrrect permissions.
180
181      Args:
182          service_client (client): The secrets manager service client
```

```
183
184         arn (string): The secret ARN or other identifier
185
186         token (string): The ClientRequestToken associated with the secret version
187
188     Raises:
189         ResourceNotFoundException: If the secret with the specified arn and stage does not exist
190
191         ValueError: If the secret is not valid JSON or valid credentials are found to login to
                the database
192
193         KeyError: If the secret json does not contain the expected keys
194
195     """
196     # Try to login with the pending secret, if it succeeds, return
197     conn = get_connection(get_secret_dict(service_client, arn, "AWSPENDING", token))
198     if conn:
199         # This is where the lambda will validate the user's permissions. Uncomment/modify the
                below lines to
200         # tailor these validations to your needs
201         try:
202             with conn.cursor() as cur:
203                 cur.execute("SELECT NOW()")
204                 conn.commit()
205         finally:
206             conn.close()
207
208         logger.info("testSecret: Successfully signed into MySQL DB with AWSPENDING secret in %s
                ." % arn)
209         return
210     else:
211         logger.error("testSecret: Unable to log into database with pending secret of secret ARN
                %s" % arn)
212         raise ValueError("Unable to log into database with pending secret of secret ARN %s" %
                arn)
213
214
215 def finish_secret(service_client, arn, token):
216     """Finish the rotation by marking the pending secret as current
217
218     This method finishes the secret rotation by staging the secret staged AWSPENDING with the
            AWSCURRENT stage.
219
220     Args:
221         service_client (client): The secrets manager service client
222
223         arn (string): The secret ARN or other identifier
224
225         token (string): The ClientRequestToken associated with the secret version
226
227     """
228     # First describe the secret to get the current version
229     metadata = service_client.describe_secret(SecretId=arn)
230     current_version = None
```

```python
231         for version in metadata["VersionIdsToStages"]:
232             if "AWSCURRENT" in metadata["VersionIdsToStages"][version]:
233                 if version == token:
234                     # The correct version is already marked as current, return
235                     logger.info("finishSecret: Version %s already marked as AWSCURRENT for %s" % (
236                         version, arn))
237                     return
238                 current_version = version
239                 break

240         # Finalize by staging the secret version current
241     service_client.update_secret_version_stage(SecretId=arn, VersionStage="AWSCURRENT",
242         MoveToVersionId=token, RemoveFromVersionId=current_version)
243     logger.info("finishSecret: Successfully set AWSCURRENT stage to version %s for secret %s." %
244         (version, arn))


245 def get_connection(secret_dict):
246     """Gets a connection to MySQL DB from a secret dictionary
247
248     This helper function tries to connect to the database grabbing connection info
249     from the secret dictionary. If successful, it returns the connection, else None
250
251     Args:
252         secret_dict (dict): The Secret Dictionary
253
254     Returns:
255         Connection: The pymysql.connections.Connection object if successful. None otherwise
256
257     Raises:
258         KeyError: If the secret json does not contain the expected keys
259
260     """
261     # Parse and validate the secret JSON string
262     port = int(secret_dict['port']) if 'port' in secret_dict else 3306
263     dbname = secret_dict['dbname'] if 'dbname' in secret_dict else None
264
265     # Try to obtain a connection to the db
266     try:
267         conn = pymysql.connect(secret_dict['host'], user=secret_dict['username'], passwd=
268             secret_dict['password'], port=port, db=dbname, connect_timeout=5)
269         return conn
270     except pymysql.OperationalError:
271         return None


273 def get_secret_dict(service_client, arn, stage, token=None):
274     """Gets the secret dictionary corresponding for the secret arn, stage, and token
275
276     This helper function gets credentials for the arn and stage passed in and returns the
277         dictionary by parsing the JSON string
278
279     Args:
280         service_client (client): The secrets manager service client
```

```
280
281        arn (string): The secret ARN or other identifier
282
283        token (string): The ClientRequestToken associated with the secret version, or None if no
                validation is desired
284
285        stage (string): The stage identifying the secret version
286
287    Returns:
288        SecretDictionary: Secret dictionary
289
290    Raises:
291        ResourceNotFoundException: If the secret with the specified arn and stage does not exist
292
293        ValueError: If the secret is not valid JSON
294
295    """
296    required_fields = ['host', 'username', 'password']
297
298    # Only do VersionId validation against the stage if a token is passed in
299    if token:
300        secret = service_client.get_secret_value(SecretId=arn, VersionId=token, VersionStage=
                stage)
301    else:
302        secret = service_client.get_secret_value(SecretId=arn, VersionStage=stage)
303    plaintext = secret['SecretString']
304    secret_dict = json.loads(plaintext)
305
306    # Run validations against the secret
307    if 'engine' not in secret_dict or secret_dict['engine'] != 'mysql':
308        raise KeyError("Database engine must be set to 'mysql' in order to use this rotation
                lambda")
309    for field in required_fields:
310        if field not in secret_dict:
311            raise KeyError("%s key is missing from secret JSON" % field)
312
313    # Parse and return the secret JSON string
314    return secret_dict
```

# Secrets Manager Lambda Rotation Template: RDS MySQL Multiple User

The following is the source code that's initially placed into the Lambda rotation function when you choose the **SecretsManagerRDSMySQLRotationMultiUser** template option from the AWS Serverless Application Repository. This template is automatically used to create the function when you enable rotation by using the Secrets Manager console. (In the console, you specify that the secret is for an Amazon RDS MySQL database, and that you want to rotate the secret using the credentials that are stored in a separate 'master user' secret.)

To create this function manually, follow the instructions at Rotating AWS Secrets Manager Secrets for Other Databases or Services and specify this template.

For more information about the rotation strategy that's implemented by this function, see Rotating AWS Secrets Manager Secrets by Alternating Between Two Existing Users.

This function is written in Python, and uses the AWS Boto3 SDK for Python.

```
1  import boto3
2  import json
3  import logging
4  import os
5  import pymysql
6
7  logger = logging.getLogger()
8  logger.setLevel(logging.INFO)
9
10
11 def lambda_handler(event, context):
12     """Secrets Manager RDS MySQL Handler
13
14     This handler uses the master-user rotation scheme to rotate an RDS MySQL user credential.
           During the first rotation, this
15     scheme logs into the database as the master user, creates a new user (appending _clone to
           the username), and grants the
16     new user all of the permissions from the user being rotated. Once the secret is in the state
           , every subsequent rotation
17     simply creates a new secret with the AWSPREVIOUS user credentials, adds any missing
           permissions that are in the current
18     secret, changes that user's password, and then marks the latest secret as AWSCURRENT.
19
20     The Secret SecretString is expected to be a JSON string with the following format:
21     {
22         'engine': <required: must be set to 'mysql'>,
23         'host': <required: instance host name>,
24         'username': <required: username>,
25         'password': <required: password>,
26         'dbname': <optional: database name>,
27         'port': <optional: if not specified, default port 3306 will be used>,
28         'masterarn': <required: the arn of the master secret which will be used to create users/
               change passwords>
29     }
30
31     Args:
32         event (dict): Lambda dictionary of event parameters. These keys must include the
               following:
```

```python
33             - SecretId: The secret ARN or identifier
34             - ClientRequestToken: The ClientRequestToken of the secret version
35             - Step: The rotation step (one of createSecret, setSecret, testSecret, or
                   finishSecret)
36
37         context (LambdaContext): The Lambda runtime information
38
39     Raises:
40         ResourceNotFoundException: If the secret with the specified arn and stage does not exist
41
42         ValueError: If the secret is not properly configured for rotation
43
44         KeyError: If the secret json does not contain the expected keys
45
46     """
47     arn = event['SecretId']
48     token = event['ClientRequestToken']
49     step = event['Step']
50
51     # Setup the client
52     service_client = boto3.client('secretsmanager', endpoint_url=os.environ['
           SECRETS_MANAGER_ENDPOINT'])
53
54     # Make sure the version is staged correctly
55     metadata = service_client.describe_secret(SecretId=arn)
56     if "RotationEnabled" in metadata and not metadata['RotationEnabled']:
57         logger.error("Secret %s is not enabled for rotation" % arn)
58         raise ValueError("Secret %s is not enabled for rotation" % arn)
59     versions = metadata['VersionIdsToStages']
60     if token not in versions:
61         logger.error("Secret version %s has no stage for rotation of secret %s." % (token, arn))
62         raise ValueError("Secret version %s has no stage for rotation of secret %s." % (token,
               arn))
63     if "AWSCURRENT" in versions[token]:
64         logger.info("Secret version %s already set as AWSCURRENT for secret %s." % (token, arn))
65         return
66     elif "AWSPENDING" not in versions[token]:
67         logger.error("Secret version %s not set as AWSPENDING for rotation of secret %s." % (
               token, arn))
68         raise ValueError("Secret version %s not set as AWSPENDING for rotation of secret %s." %
               (token, arn))
69
70     # Call the appropriate step
71     if step == "createSecret":
72         create_secret(service_client, arn, token)
73
74     elif step == "setSecret":
75         set_secret(service_client, arn, token)
76
77     elif step == "testSecret":
78         test_secret(service_client, arn, token)
79
80     elif step == "finishSecret":
81         finish_secret(service_client, arn, token)
```

```
82
83      else:
84          logger.error("lambda_handler: Invalid step parameter %s for secret %s" % (step, arn))
85          raise ValueError("Invalid step parameter %s for secret %s" % (step, arn))
86
87
88  def create_secret(service_client, arn, token):
89      """Generate a new secret
90
91      This method first checks for the existence of a secret for the passed in token. If one does
              not exist, it will generate a
92      new secret and save it using the passed in token.
93
94      Args:
95          service_client (client): The secrets manager service client
96
97          arn (string): The secret ARN or other identifier
98
99          token (string): The ClientRequestToken associated with the secret version
100
101     Raises:
102         ValueError: If the current secret is not valid JSON
103
104         KeyError: If the secret json does not contain the expected keys
105
106     """
107     # Make sure the current secret exists
108     current_dict = get_secret_dict(service_client, arn, "AWSCURRENT")
109
110     # Now try to get the secret version, if that fails, put a new secret
111     try:
112         get_secret_dict(service_client, arn, "AWSPENDING", token)
113         logger.info("createSecret: Successfully retrieved secret for %s." % arn)
114     except service_client.exceptions.ResourceNotFoundException:
115         # Get the alternate username swapping between the original user and the user with _clone
                  appended to it
116         current_dict['username'] = get_alt_username(current_dict['username'])
117
118         # Generate a random password
119         passwd = service_client.get_random_password(ExcludeCharacters='/@"\'\\')
120         current_dict['password'] = passwd['RandomPassword']
121
122         # Put the secret
123         service_client.put_secret_value(SecretId=arn, ClientRequestToken=token, SecretString=
                  json.dumps(current_dict), VersionStages=['AWSPENDING'])
124         logger.info("createSecret: Successfully put secret for ARN %s and version %s." % (arn,
                  token))
125
126
127 def set_secret(service_client, arn, token):
128     """Set the pending secret in the database
129
130     This method tries to login to the database with the AWSPENDING secret and returns on success
              . If that fails, it
```

```
131    tries to login with the master credentials from the masterarn in the current secret. If this
           succeeds, it adds all
132    grants for AWSCURRENT user to the AWSPENDING user, creating the user and/or setting the
           password in the process.
133    Else, it throws a ValueError.
134
135    Args:
136        service_client (client): The secrets manager service client
137
138        arn (string): The secret ARN or other identifier
139
140        token (string): The ClientRequestToken associated with the secret version
141
142    Raises:
143        ResourceNotFoundException: If the secret with the specified arn and stage does not exist
144
145        ValueError: If the secret is not valid JSON or master credentials could not be used to
               login to DB
146
147        KeyError: If the secret json does not contain the expected keys
148
149    """
150    # First try to login with the pending secret, if it succeeds, return
151    pending_dict = get_secret_dict(service_client, arn, "AWSPENDING", token)
152    conn = get_connection(pending_dict)
153    if conn:
154        conn.close()
155        logger.info("setSecret: AWSPENDING secret is already set as password in MySQL DB for
               secret arn %s." % arn)
156        return
157
158    # Before we do anything with the secret, make sure the AWSCURRENT secret is valid by logging
           in to the db
159    current_dict = get_secret_dict(service_client, arn, "AWSCURRENT")
160    conn = get_connection(current_dict)
161    if not conn:
162        logger.error("setSecret: Unable to log into database using current credentials for
               secret %s" % arn)
163        raise ValueError("Unable to log into database using current credentials for secret %s" %
               arn)
164    conn.close()
165
166    # Now get the master arn from the current secret
167    master_arn = current_dict['masterarn']
168    master_dict = get_secret_dict(service_client, master_arn, "AWSCURRENT")
169    if current_dict['host'] != master_dict['host']:
170        logger.warn("setSecret: Master database host %s is not the same host as current %s" % (
               master_dict['host'], current_dict['host']))
171
172    # Now log into the database with the master credentials
173    conn = get_connection(master_dict)
174    if not conn:
175        logger.error("setSecret: Unable to log into database using credentials in master secret
               %s" % master_arn)
```

```
176          raise ValueError("Unable to log into database using credentials in master secret %s" %
                 master_arn)
177
178      # Now set the password to the pending password
179      try:
180          with conn.cursor() as cur:
181              # List the grants on the current user and add them to the pending user.
182              # This also creates the user if it does not already exist
183              cur.execute("SHOW GRANTS FOR %s", current_dict['username'])
184              for row in cur.fetchall():
185                  grant = row[0].split(' TO ')
186                  new_grant = "%s TO %s" % (grant[0], pending_dict['username'])
187                  cur.execute(new_grant + " IDENTIFIED BY %s", pending_dict['password'])
188              conn.commit()
189              logger.info("setSecret: Successfully set password for %s in MySQL DB for secret arn
                     %s." % (pending_dict['username'], arn))
190      finally:
191          conn.close()
192
193
194  def test_secret(service_client, arn, token):
195      """Test the pending secret against the database
196
197      This method tries to log into the database with the secrets staged with AWSPENDING and runs
198      a permissions check to ensure the user has the correct permissions.
199
200      Args:
201          service_client (client): The secrets manager service client
202
203          arn (string): The secret ARN or other identifier
204
205          token (string): The ClientRequestToken associated with the secret version
206
207      Raises:
208          ResourceNotFoundException: If the secret with the specified arn and stage does not exist
209
210          ValueError: If the secret is not valid JSON or pending credentials could not be used to
                 login to the database
211
212          KeyError: If the secret json does not contain the expected keys
213
214      """
215      # Try to login with the pending secret, if it succeeds, return
216      conn = get_connection(get_secret_dict(service_client, arn, "AWSPENDING", token))
217      if conn:
218          # This is where the lambda will validate the user's permissions. Modify the below lines
                 to
219          # tailor these validations to your needs
220          try:
221              with conn.cursor() as cur:
222                  cur.execute("SELECT NOW()")
223                  conn.commit()
224          finally:
225              conn.close()
```

128

```
226
227         logger.info("testSecret: Successfully signed into MySQL DB with AWSPENDING secret in %s
               ." % arn)
228         return
229     else:
230         logger.error("testSecret: Unable to log into database with pending secret of secret ARN
               %s" % arn)
231         raise ValueError("Unable to log into database with pending secret of secret ARN %s" %
               arn)
232
233
234 def finish_secret(service_client, arn, token):
235     """Finish the rotation by marking the pending secret as current
236
237     This method moves the secret from the AWSPENDING stage to the AWSCURRENT stage.
238
239     Args:
240         service_client (client): The secrets manager service client
241
242         arn (string): The secret ARN or other identifier
243
244         token (string): The ClientRequestToken associated with the secret version
245
246     Raises:
247         ResourceNotFoundException: If the secret with the specified arn and stage does not exist
248
249     """
250     # First describe the secret to get the current version
251     metadata = service_client.describe_secret(SecretId=arn)
252     current_version = None
253     for version in metadata["VersionIdsToStages"]:
254         if "AWSCURRENT" in metadata["VersionIdsToStages"][version]:
255             if version == token:
256                 # The correct version is already marked as current, return
257                 logger.info("finishSecret: Version %s already marked as AWSCURRENT for %s" % (
                       version, arn))
258                 return
259             current_version = version
260             break
261
262     # Finalize by staging the secret version current
263     service_client.update_secret_version_stage(SecretId=arn, VersionStage="AWSCURRENT",
               MoveToVersionId=token, RemoveFromVersionId=current_version)
264     logger.info("finishSecret: Successfully set AWSCURRENT stage to version %s for secret %s." %
               (version, arn))
265
266
267 def get_connection(secret_dict):
268     """Gets a connection to MySQL DB from a secret dictionary
269
270     This helper function tries to connect to the database grabbing connection info
271     from the secret dictionary. If successful, it returns the connection, else None
272
273     Args:
```

```
274          secret_dict (dict): The Secret Dictionary
275
276      Returns:
277          Connection: The pymysql.connections.Connection object if successful. None otherwise
278
279      Raises:
280          KeyError: If the secret json does not contain the expected keys
281
282      """
283      port = int(secret_dict['port']) if 'port' in secret_dict else 3306
284      dbname = secret_dict['dbname'] if 'dbname' in secret_dict else None
285
286      # Try to obtain a connection to the db
287      try:
288          conn = pymysql.connect(secret_dict['host'], user=secret_dict['username'], passwd=
                  secret_dict['password'], port=port, db=dbname, connect_timeout=5)
289          return conn
290      except pymysql.OperationalError:
291          return None
292
293
294  def get_secret_dict(service_client, arn, stage, token=None):
295      """Gets the secret dictionary corresponding for the secret arn, stage, and token
296
297      This helper function gets credentials for the arn and stage passed in and returns the
              dictionary by parsing the JSON string
298
299      Args:
300          service_client (client): The secrets manager service client
301
302          arn (string): The secret ARN or other identifier
303
304          token (string): The ClientRequestToken associated with the secret version, or None if no
                  validation is desired
305
306          stage (string): The stage identifying the secret version
307
308      Returns:
309          SecretDictionary: Secret dictionary
310
311      Raises:
312          ResourceNotFoundException: If the secret with the specified arn and stage does not exist
313
314          ValueError: If the secret is not valid JSON
315
316      """
317      required_fields = ['host', 'username', 'password']
318
319      # Only do VersionId validation against the stage if a token is passed in
320      if token:
321          secret = service_client.get_secret_value(SecretId=arn, VersionId=token, VersionStage=
                  stage)
322      else:
323          secret = service_client.get_secret_value(SecretId=arn, VersionStage=stage)
```

```
324        plaintext = secret['SecretString']
325        secret_dict = json.loads(plaintext)
326
327        # Run validations against the secret
328        if 'engine' not in secret_dict or secret_dict['engine'] != 'mysql':
329            raise KeyError("Database engine must be set to 'mysql' in order to use this rotation
                   lambda")
330        for field in required_fields:
331            if field not in secret_dict:
332                raise KeyError("%s key is missing from secret JSON" % field)
333
334        # Parse and return the secret JSON string
335        return secret_dict
336
337
338 def get_alt_username(current_username):
339     """Gets the alternate username for the current_username passed in
340
341     This helper function gets the username for the alternate user based on the passed in current
               username.
342
343     Args:
344         current_username (client): The current username
345
346     Returns:
347         AlternateUsername: Alternate username
348
349     Raises:
350         ValueError: If the new username length would exceed the maximum allowed
351
352     """
353     clone_suffix = "_clone"
354     if current_username.endswith(clone_suffix):
355         return current_username[:(len(clone_suffix) * -1)]
356     else:
357         new_username = current_username + clone_suffix
358         if len(new_username) > 16:
359             raise ValueError("Unable to clone user, username length with _clone appended would
                       exceed 16 characters")
360         return new_username
```

# Secrets Manager Lambda Rotation Template: RDS PostgreSQL Single User

The following is the source code that's initially placed into the Lambda rotation function when you choose the **SecretsManagerRDSPostgreSQLRotationSingleUser** template option from the AWS Serverless Application Repository.

For more information about the rotation strategy that's implemented by this function, see Rotating AWS Secrets Manager Secrets for One User with a Single Password.

This function is written in Python, and uses the AWS Boto3 SDK for Python.

```
1  import boto3
2  import json
3  import logging
4  import os
5  import pg
6  import pgdb
7
8  logger = logging.getLogger()
9  logger.setLevel(logging.INFO)
10
11
12 def lambda_handler(event, context):
13     """Secrets Manager RDS PostgreSQL Handler
14
15     This handler uses the single-user rotation scheme to rotate an RDS PostgreSQL user
           credential. This rotation
16     scheme logs into the database as the user and rotates the user's own password, immediately
           invalidating the
17     user's previous password.
18
19     The Secret SecretString is expected to be a JSON string with the following format:
20     {
21         'engine': &lt;required: must be set to 'postgres'>,
22         'host': &lt;required: instance host name>,
23         'username': &lt;required: username>,
24         'password': &lt;required: password>,
25         'dbname': &lt;optional: database name, default to 'postgres'>,
26         'port': &lt;optional: if not specified, default port 5432 will be used>
27     }
28
29     Args:
30         event (dict): Lambda dictionary of event parameters. These keys must include the
               following:
31             - SecretId: The secret ARN or identifier
32             - ClientRequestToken: The ClientRequestToken of the secret version
33             - Step: The rotation step (one of createSecret, setSecret, testSecret, or
                   finishSecret)
34
35         context (LambdaContext): The Lambda runtime information
36
37     Raises:
38         ResourceNotFoundException: If the secret with the specified arn and stage does not exist
39
```

```python
40          ValueError: If the secret is not properly configured for rotation
41
42          KeyError: If the secret json does not contain the expected keys
43
44      """
45      arn = event['SecretId']
46      token = event['ClientRequestToken']
47      step = event['Step']
48
49      # Setup the client
50      service_client = boto3.client('secretsmanager', endpoint_url=os.environ['
            SECRETS_MANAGER_ENDPOINT'])
51
52      # Make sure the version is staged correctly
53      metadata = service_client.describe_secret(SecretId=arn)
54      if "RotationEnabled" in metadata and not metadata['RotationEnabled']:
55          logger.error("Secret %s is not enabled for rotation" % arn)
56          raise ValueError("Secret %s is not enabled for rotation" % arn)
57      versions = metadata['VersionIdsToStages']
58      if token not in versions:
59          logger.error("Secret version %s has no stage for rotation of secret %s." % (token, arn))
60          raise ValueError("Secret version %s has no stage for rotation of secret %s." % (token,
                arn))
61      if "AWSCURRENT" in versions[token]:
62          logger.info("Secret version %s already set as AWSCURRENT for secret %s." % (token, arn))
63          return
64      elif "AWSPENDING" not in versions[token]:
65          logger.error("Secret version %s not set as AWSPENDING for rotation of secret %s." % (
                token, arn))
66          raise ValueError("Secret version %s not set as AWSPENDING for rotation of secret %s." %
                (token, arn))
67
68      # Call the appropriate step
69      if step == "createSecret":
70          create_secret(service_client, arn, token)
71
72      elif step == "setSecret":
73          set_secret(service_client, arn, token)
74
75      elif step == "testSecret":
76          test_secret(service_client, arn, token)
77
78      elif step == "finishSecret":
79          finish_secret(service_client, arn, token)
80
81      else:
82          logger.error("lambda_handler: Invalid step parameter %s for secret %s" % (step, arn))
83          raise ValueError("Invalid step parameter %s for secret %s" % (step, arn))
84
85
86  def create_secret(service_client, arn, token):
87      """Generate a new secret
88
89      This method first checks for the existence of a secret for the passed in token. If one does
```

```
 90    not exist, it will generate a
       new secret and put it with the passed in token.

 91

 92    Args:

 93        service_client (client): The secrets manager service client

 94

 95        arn (string): The secret ARN or other identifier

 96

 97        token (string): The ClientRequestToken associated with the secret version

 98

 99    Raises:

100        ValueError: If the current secret is not valid JSON

101

102        KeyError: If the secret json does not contain the expected keys

103

104    """

105    # Make sure the current secret exists

106    current_dict = get_secret_dict(service_client, arn, "AWSCURRENT")

107

108    # Now try to get the secret version, if that fails, put a new secret

109    try:

110        get_secret_dict(service_client, arn, "AWSPENDING", token)

111        logger.info("createSecret: Successfully retrieved secret for %s." % arn)

112    except service_client.exceptions.ResourceNotFoundException:

113        # Generate a random password

114        passwd = service_client.get_random_password(ExcludeCharacters='/@"\'\\')

115        current_dict['password'] = passwd['RandomPassword']

116

117        # Put the secret

118        service_client.put_secret_value(SecretId=arn, ClientRequestToken=token, SecretString=
               json.dumps(current_dict), VersionStages=['AWSPENDING'])

119        logger.info("createSecret: Successfully put secret for ARN %s and version %s." % (arn,
               token))

120

121

122 def set_secret(service_client, arn, token):

123    """Set the pending secret in the database

124

125    This method tries to login to the database with the AWSPENDING secret and returns on success
           . If that fails, it

126    tries to login with the AWSCURRENT and AWSPREVIOUS secrets. If either one succeeds, it sets
           the AWSPENDING password

127    as the user password in the database. Else, it throws a ValueError.

128

129    Args:

130        service_client (client): The secrets manager service client

131

132        arn (string): The secret ARN or other identifier

133

134        token (string): The ClientRequestToken associated with the secret version

135

136    Raises:

137        ResourceNotFoundException: If the secret with the specified arn and stage does not exist

138
```

```
139          ValueError: If the secret is not valid JSON or valid credentials are found to login to
                 the database

140
141          KeyError: If the secret json does not contain the expected keys

142
143      """
144      # First try to login with the pending secret, if it succeeds, return
145      pending_dict = get_secret_dict(service_client, arn, "AWSPENDING", token)
146      conn = get_connection(pending_dict)
147      if conn:
148          conn.close()
149          logger.info("setSecret: AWSPENDING secret is already set as password in PostgreSQL DB
                 for secret arn %s." % arn)
150          return

151
152      # Now try the current password
153      conn = get_connection(get_secret_dict(service_client, arn, "AWSCURRENT"))
154      if not conn:
155          # If both current and pending do not work, try previous
156          try:
157              conn = get_connection(get_secret_dict(service_client, arn, "AWSPREVIOUS"))
158          except service_client.exceptions.ResourceNotFoundException:
159              conn = None

160
161      # If we still don't have a connection, raise a ValueError
162      if not conn:
163          logger.error("setSecret: Unable to log into database with previous, current, or pending
                 secret of secret arn %s" % arn)
164          raise ValueError("Unable to log into database with previous, current, or pending secret
                 of secret arn %s" % arn)

165
166      # Now set the password to the pending password
167      try:
168          with conn.cursor() as cur:
169              alter_role = "ALTER USER %s" % pending_dict['username']
170              cur.execute(alter_role + " WITH PASSWORD %s", (pending_dict['password'],))
171              conn.commit()
172              logger.info("setSecret: Successfully set password for user %s in PostgreSQL DB for
                     secret arn %s." % (pending_dict['username'], arn))
173      finally:
174          conn.close()

175
176
177  def test_secret(service_client, arn, token):
178      """Test the pending secret against the database

179
180      This method tries to log into the database with the secrets staged with AWSPENDING and runs
181      a permissions check to ensure the user has the corrrect permissions.

182
183      Args:
184          service_client (client): The secrets manager service client

185
186          arn (string): The secret ARN or other identifier

187
```

```
188        token (string): The ClientRequestToken associated with the secret version
189
190    Raises:
191        ResourceNotFoundException: If the secret with the specified arn and stage does not exist
192
193        ValueError: If the secret is not valid JSON or valid credentials are found to login to
               the database
194
195        KeyError: If the secret json does not contain the expected keys
196
197    """
198    # Try to login with the pending secret, if it succeeds, return
199    conn = get_connection(get_secret_dict(service_client, arn, "AWSPENDING", token))
200    if conn:
201        # This is where the lambda will validate the user's permissions. Uncomment/modify the
               below lines to
202        # tailor these validations to your needs
203        try:
204            with conn.cursor() as cur:
205                cur.execute("SELECT NOW()")
206                conn.commit()
207        finally:
208            conn.close()
209
210        logger.info("testSecret: Successfully signed into PostgreSQL DB with AWSPENDING secret
               in %s." % arn)
211        return
212    else:
213        logger.error("testSecret: Unable to log into database with pending secret of secret ARN
               %s" % arn)
214        raise ValueError("Unable to log into database with pending secret of secret ARN %s" %
               arn)
215
216
217 def finish_secret(service_client, arn, token):
218    """Finish the rotation by marking the pending secret as current
219
220    This method finishes the secret rotation by staging the secret staged AWSPENDING with the
           AWSCURRENT stage.
221
222    Args:
223        service_client (client): The secrets manager service client
224
225        arn (string): The secret ARN or other identifier
226
227        token (string): The ClientRequestToken associated with the secret version
228
229    """
230    # First describe the secret to get the current version
231    metadata = service_client.describe_secret(SecretId=arn)
232    current_version = None
233    for version in metadata["VersionIdsToStages"]:
234        if "AWSCURRENT" in metadata["VersionIdsToStages"][version]:
235            if version == token:
```

```
236              # The correct version is already marked as current, return
237              logger.info("finishSecret: Version %s already marked as AWSCURRENT for %s" % (
                     version, arn))
238              return
239          current_version = version
240          break
241
242      # Finalize by staging the secret version current
243      service_client.update_secret_version_stage(SecretId=arn, VersionStage="AWSCURRENT",
             MoveToVersionId=token, RemoveFromVersionId=current_version)
244      logger.info("finishSecret: Successfully set AWSCURRENT stage to version %s for secret %s." %
             (version, arn))
245
246
247  def get_connection(secret_dict):
248      """Gets a connection to PostgreSQL DB from a secret dictionary
249
250      This helper function tries to connect to the database grabbing connection info
251      from the secret dictionary. If successful, it returns the connection, else None
252
253      Args:
254          secret_dict (dict): The Secret Dictionary
255
256      Returns:
257          Connection: The pgdb.Connection object if successful. None otherwise
258
259      Raises:
260          KeyError: If the secret json does not contain the expected keys
261
262      """
263      # Parse and validate the secret JSON string
264      port = int(secret_dict['port']) if 'port' in secret_dict else 5432
265      dbname = secret_dict['dbname'] if 'dbname' in secret_dict else "postgres"
266
267      # Try to obtain a connection to the db
268      try:
269          conn = pgdb.connect(host=secret_dict['host'], user=secret_dict['username'], password=
              secret_dict['password'], database=dbname, port=port, connect_timeout=5)
270          return conn
271      except pg.InternalError:
272          return None
273
274
275  def get_secret_dict(service_client, arn, stage, token=None):
276      """Gets the secret dictionary corresponding for the secret arn, stage, and token
277
278      This helper function gets credentials for the arn and stage passed in and returns the
              dictionary by parsing the JSON string
279
280      Args:
281          service_client (client): The secrets manager service client
282
283          arn (string): The secret ARN or other identifier
284
```

```
285        token (string): The ClientRequestToken associated with the secret version, or None if no
               validation is desired
286
287        stage (string): The stage identifying the secret version
288
289    Returns:
290        SecretDictionary: Secret dictionary
291
292    Raises:
293        ResourceNotFoundException: If the secret with the specified arn and stage does not exist
294
295        ValueError: If the secret is not valid JSON
296
297    """
298    required_fields = ['host', 'username', 'password']
299
300    # Only do VersionId validation against the stage if a token is passed in
301    if token:
302        secret = service_client.get_secret_value(SecretId=arn, VersionId=token, VersionStage=
               stage)
303    else:
304        secret = service_client.get_secret_value(SecretId=arn, VersionStage=stage)
305    plaintext = secret['SecretString']
306    secret_dict = json.loads(plaintext)
307
308    # Run validations against the secret
309    if 'engine' not in secret_dict or secret_dict['engine'] != 'postgres':
310        raise KeyError("Database engine must be set to 'postgres' in order to use this rotation
               lambda")
311    for field in required_fields:
312        if field not in secret_dict:
313            raise KeyError("%s key is missing from secret JSON" % field)
314
315    # Parse and return the secret JSON string
316    return secret_dict
```

# Secrets Manager Lambda Rotation Template: RDS PostgreSQL Multiple User

The following is the source code that's initially placed into the Lambda rotation function when you choose the **SecretsManagerRDSPostgreSQLRotationMultiUser** template option from the AWS Serverless Application Repository. This template is automatically used to create the function when you enable rotation by using the Secrets Manager console. (In the console, you specify that the secret is for an Amazon RDS PostgreSQL database, and that you want to rotate the secret using the credentials that are stored in a separate 'master user' secret.)

To create this function manually, follow the instructions at Rotating AWS Secrets Manager Secrets for Other Databases or Services and specify this template.

For more information about the rotation strategy that's implemented by this function, see Rotating AWS Secrets Manager Secrets by Alternating Between Two Existing Users.

This function is written in Python, and uses the AWS Boto3 SDK for Python.

```
1  import boto3
2  import json
3  import logging
4  import os
5  import pg
6  import pgdb
7
8  logger = logging.getLogger()
9  logger.setLevel(logging.INFO)
10
11
12 def lambda_handler(event, context):
13     """Secrets Manager RDS PostgreSQL Handler
14
15     This handler uses the master-user rotation scheme to rotate an RDS PostgreSQL user
             credential. During the first rotation, this
16     scheme logs into the database as the master user, creates a new user (appending _clone to
             the username), and grants the
17     new user all of the permissions from the user being rotated. Once the secret is in the state
             , every subsequent rotation
18     simply creates a new secret with the AWSPREVIOUS user credentials, adds any missing
             permissions that are in the current
19     secret, changes that user's password, and then marks the latest secret as AWSCURRENT.
20
21     The Secret SecretString is expected to be a JSON string with the following format:
22     {
23         'engine': <required: must be set to 'postgres'>,
24         'host': <required: instance host name>,
25         'username': <required: username>,
26         'password': <required: password>,
27         'dbname': <optional: database name, default to 'postgres'>,
28         'port': <optional: if not specified, default port 5432 will be used>,
29         'masterarn': <required: the arn of the master secret which will be used to create
                 users/change passwords>
30     }
31
32     Args:
```

```
33      event (dict): Lambda dictionary of event parameters. These keys must include the
            following:
34          - SecretId: The secret ARN or identifier
35          - ClientRequestToken: The ClientRequestToken of the secret version
36          - Step: The rotation step (one of createSecret, setSecret, testSecret, or
              finishSecret)
37
38      context (LambdaContext): The Lambda runtime information
39
40  Raises:
41      ResourceNotFoundException: If the secret with the specified arn and stage does not exist
42
43      ValueError: If the secret is not properly configured for rotation
44
45      KeyError: If the secret json does not contain the expected keys
46
47      """
48  arn = event['SecretId']
49  token = event['ClientRequestToken']
50  step = event['Step']
51
52  # Setup the client
53  service_client = boto3.client('secretsmanager', endpoint_url=os.environ['
        SECRETS_MANAGER_ENDPOINT'])
54
55  # Make sure the version is staged correctly
56  metadata = service_client.describe_secret(SecretId=arn)
57  if "RotationEnabled" in metadata and not metadata['RotationEnabled']:
58      logger.error("Secret %s is not enabled for rotation" % arn)
59      raise ValueError("Secret %s is not enabled for rotation" % arn)
60  versions = metadata['VersionIdsToStages']
61  if token not in versions:
62      logger.error("Secret version %s has no stage for rotation of secret %s." % (token, arn))
63      raise ValueError("Secret version %s has no stage for rotation of secret %s." % (token,
          arn))
64  if "AWSCURRENT" in versions[token]:
65      logger.info("Secret version %s already set as AWSCURRENT for secret %s." % (token, arn))
66      return
67  elif "AWSPENDING" not in versions[token]:
68      logger.error("Secret version %s not set as AWSPENDING for rotation of secret %s." % (
          token, arn))
69      raise ValueError("Secret version %s not set as AWSPENDING for rotation of secret %s." %
          (token, arn))
70
71  # Call the appropriate step
72  if step == "createSecret":
73      create_secret(service_client, arn, token)
74
75  elif step == "setSecret":
76      set_secret(service_client, arn, token)
77
78  elif step == "testSecret":
79      test_secret(service_client, arn, token)
80
```

```
81    elif step == "finishSecret":
82        finish_secret(service_client, arn, token)
83
84    else:
85        logger.error("lambda_handler: Invalid step parameter %s for secret %s" % (step, arn))
86        raise ValueError("Invalid step parameter %s for secret %s" % (step, arn))
87
88
89 def create_secret(service_client, arn, token):
90     """Generate a new secret
91
92     This method first checks for the existence of a secret for the passed in token. If one does
           not exist, it will generate a
93     new secret and put it with the passed in token.
94
95     Args:
96         service_client (client): The secrets manager service client
97
98         arn (string): The secret ARN or other identifier
99
100        token (string): The ClientRequestToken associated with the secret version
101
102    Raises:
103        ValueError: If the current secret is not valid JSON
104
105        KeyError: If the secret json does not contain the expected keys
106
107    """
108    # Make sure the current secret exists
109    current_dict = get_secret_dict(service_client, arn, "AWSCURRENT")
110
111    # Now try to get the secret version, if that fails, put a new secret
112    try:
113        get_secret_dict(service_client, arn, "AWSPENDING", token)
114        logger.info("createSecret: Successfully retrieved secret for %s." % arn)
115    except service_client.exceptions.ResourceNotFoundException:
116        # Get the alternate username swapping between the original user and the user with _clone
               appended to it
117        current_dict['username'] = get_alt_username(current_dict['username'])
118
119        # Generate a random password
120        passwd = service_client.get_random_password(ExcludeCharacters='/@"\'\\')
121        current_dict['password'] = passwd['RandomPassword']
122
123        # Put the secret
124        service_client.put_secret_value(SecretId=arn, ClientRequestToken=token, SecretString=
               json.dumps(current_dict), VersionStages=['AWSPENDING'])
125        logger.info("createSecret: Successfully put secret for ARN %s and version %s." % (arn,
               token))
126
127
128 def set_secret(service_client, arn, token):
129     """Set the pending secret in the database
130
```

```
131    This method tries to login to the database with the AWSPENDING secret and returns on success
           . If that fails, it
132    tries to login with the master credentials from the masterarn in the current secret. If this
               succeeds, it adds all
133    grants for AWSCURRENT user to the AWSPENDING user, creating the user and/or setting the
               password in the process.
134    Else, it throws a ValueError.
135
136    Args:
137        service_client (client): The secrets manager service client
138
139        arn (string): The secret ARN or other identifier
140
141        token (string): The ClientRequestToken associated with the secret version
142
143    Raises:
144        ResourceNotFoundException: If the secret with the specified arn and stage does not exist
145
146        ValueError: If the secret is not valid JSON or master credentials could not be used to
               login to DB
147
148        KeyError: If the secret json does not contain the expected keys
149
150    """
151    # First try to login with the pending secret, if it succeeds, return
152    pending_dict = get_secret_dict(service_client, arn, "AWSPENDING", token)
153    conn = get_connection(pending_dict)
154    if conn:
155        conn.close()
156        logger.info("setSecret: AWSPENDING secret is already set as password in PostgreSQL DB
               for secret arn %s." % arn)
157        return
158
159    # Before we do anything with the secret, make sure the AWSCURRENT secret is valid by logging
           in to the db
160    current_dict = get_secret_dict(service_client, arn, "AWSCURRENT")
161    conn = get_connection(current_dict)
162    if not conn:
163        logger.error("setSecret: Unable to log into database using current credentials for
               secret %s" % arn)
164        raise ValueError("Unable to log into database using current credentials for secret %s" %
               arn)
165    conn.close()
166
167    # Now get the master arn from the current secret
168    master_arn = current_dict['masterarn']
169    master_dict = get_secret_dict(service_client, master_arn, "AWSCURRENT")
170    if current_dict['host'] != master_dict['host']:
171        logger.warn("setSecret: Master database host %s is not the same host as current %s" % (
               master_dict['host'], current_dict['host']))
172
173    # Now log into the database with the master credentials
174    conn = get_connection(master_dict)
175    if not conn:
```

```
176        logger.error("setSecret: Unable to log into database using credentials in master secret
               %s" % master_arn)
177        raise ValueError("Unable to log into database using credentials in master secret %s" %
               master_arn)
178
179    # Now set the password to the pending password
180    try:
181        with conn.cursor() as cur:
182            # Check if the user exists, if not create it and grant it all permissions from the
                   current role
183            # If the user exists, just update the password
184            cur.execute("SELECT 1 FROM pg_roles where rolname = %s", (pending_dict['username'],)
                   )
185            if len(cur.fetchall()) == 0:
186                create_role = "CREATE ROLE %s" % pending_dict['username']
187                cur.execute(create_role + " WITH LOGIN PASSWORD %s", (pending_dict['password'],)
                       )
188                cur.execute("GRANT %s TO %s" % (current_dict['username'], pending_dict['username
                       ']))
189            else:
190                alter_role = "ALTER USER %s" % pending_dict['username']
191                cur.execute(alter_role + " WITH PASSWORD %s", (pending_dict['password'],))
192
193            conn.commit()
194            logger.info("setSecret: Successfully created user %s in PostgreSQL DB for secret arn
                   %s." % (pending_dict['username'], arn))
195    finally:
196        conn.close()
197
198
199 def test_secret(service_client, arn, token):
200    """Test the pending secret against the database
201
202    This method tries to log into the database with the secrets staged with AWSPENDING and runs
203    a permissions check to ensure the user has the correct permissions.
204
205    Args:
206        service_client (client): The secrets manager service client
207
208        arn (string): The secret ARN or other identifier
209
210        token (string): The ClientRequestToken associated with the secret version
211
212    Raises:
213        ResourceNotFoundException: If the secret with the specified arn and stage does not exist
214
215        ValueError: If the secret is not valid JSON or pending credentials could not be used to
               login to the database
216
217        KeyError: If the secret json does not contain the expected keys
218
219    """
220    # Try to login with the pending secret, if it succeeds, return
221    conn = get_connection(get_secret_dict(service_client, arn, "AWSPENDING", token))
```

```
222     if conn:
223         # This is where the lambda will validate the user's permissions. Uncomment/modify the
                below lines to
224         # tailor these validations to your needs
225         try:
226             with conn.cursor() as cur:
227                 cur.execute("SELECT NOW()")
228                 conn.commit()
229         finally:
230             conn.close()
231
232         logger.info("testSecret: Successfully signed into PostgreSQL DB with AWSPENDING secret
                in %s." % arn)
233         return
234     else:
235         logger.error("testSecret: Unable to log into database with pending secret of secret ARN
                %s" % arn)
236         raise ValueError("Unable to log into database with pending secret of secret ARN %s" %
                arn)
237
238
239 def finish_secret(service_client, arn, token):
240     """Finish the rotation by marking the pending secret as current
241
242     This method moves the secret from the AWSPENDING stage to the AWSCURRENT stage.
243
244     Args:
245         service_client (client): The secrets manager service client
246
247         arn (string): The secret ARN or other identifier
248
249         token (string): The ClientRequestToken associated with the secret version
250
251     Raises:
252         ResourceNotFoundException: If the secret with the specified arn does not exist
253
254     """
255     # First describe the secret to get the current version
256     metadata = service_client.describe_secret(SecretId=arn)
257     current_version = None
258     for version in metadata["VersionIdsToStages"]:
259         if "AWSCURRENT" in metadata["VersionIdsToStages"][version]:
260             if version == token:
261                 # The correct version is already marked as current, return
262                 logger.info("finishSecret: Version %s already marked as AWSCURRENT for %s" % (
                        version, arn))
263                 return
264             current_version = version
265             break
266
267     # Finalize by staging the secret version current
268     service_client.update_secret_version_stage(SecretId=arn, VersionStage="AWSCURRENT",
            MoveToVersionId=token, RemoveFromVersionId=current_version)
269     logger.info("finishSecret: Successfully set AWSCURRENT stage to version %s for secret %s." %
```

```
          (version, arn))
270
271
272  def get_connection(secret_dict):
273      """Gets a connection to PostgreSQL DB from a secret dictionary
274
275      This helper function tries to connect to the database grabbing connection info
276      from the secret dictionary. If successful, it returns the connection, else None
277
278      Args:
279          secret_dict (dict): The Secret Dictionary
280
281      Returns:
282          Connection: The pgdb.Connection object if successful. None otherwise
283
284      Raises:
285          KeyError: If the secret json does not contain the expected keys
286
287      """
288      # Parse and validate the secret JSON string
289      port = int(secret_dict['port']) if 'port' in secret_dict else 5432
290      dbname = secret_dict['dbname'] if 'dbname' in secret_dict else "postgres"
291
292      # Try to obtain a connection to the db
293      try:
294          conn = pgdb.connect(host=secret_dict['host'], user=secret_dict['username'], password=
                 secret_dict['password'], database=dbname, port=port, connect_timeout=5)
295          return conn
296      except pg.InternalError:
297          return None
298
299
300  def get_secret_dict(service_client, arn, stage, token=None):
301      """Gets the secret dictionary corresponding for the secret arn, stage, and token
302
303      This helper function gets credentials for the arn and stage passed in and returns the
             dictionary by parsing the JSON string
304
305      Args:
306          service_client (client): The secrets manager service client
307
308          arn (string): The secret ARN or other identifier
309
310          token (string): The ClientRequestToken associated with the secret version, or None if no
                 validation is desired
311
312          stage (string): The stage identifying the secret version
313
314      Returns:
315          SecretDictionary: Secret dictionary
316
317      Raises:
318          ResourceNotFoundException: If the secret with the specified arn and stage does not exist
319
```

```
320            ValueError: If the secret is not valid JSON
321
322            KeyError: If the secret json does not contain the expected keys
323
324        """
325        required_fields = ['host', 'username', 'password']
326
327        # Only do VersionId validation against the stage if a token is passed in
328        if token:
329            secret = service_client.get_secret_value(SecretId=arn, VersionId=token, VersionStage=
                   stage)
330        else:
331            secret = service_client.get_secret_value(SecretId=arn, VersionStage=stage)
332        plaintext = secret['SecretString']
333        secret_dict = json.loads(plaintext)
334
335        # Run validations against the secret
336        if 'engine' not in secret_dict or secret_dict['engine'] != 'postgres':
337            raise KeyError("Database engine must be set to 'postgres' in order to use this rotation
                   lambda")
338        for field in required_fields:
339            if field not in secret_dict:
340                raise KeyError("%s key is missing from secret JSON" % field)
341
342        # Parse and return the secret JSON string
343        return secret_dict
344
345
346 def get_alt_username(current_username):
347     """Gets the alternate username for the current_username passed in
348
349     This helper function gets the username for the alternate user based on the passed in current
                   username.
350
351     Args:
352         current_username (client): The current username
353
354     Returns:
355         AlternateUsername: Alternate username
356
357     Raises:
358         ValueError: If the new username length would exceed the maximum allowed
359
360     """
361     clone_suffix = "_clone"
362     if current_username.endswith(clone_suffix):
363         return current_username[:(len(clone_suffix) * -1)]
364     else:
365         new_username = current_username + clone_suffix
366         if len(new_username) > 63:
367             raise ValueError("Unable to clone user, username length with _clone appended would
                   exceed 63 characters")
368         return new_username
```

# AWS Managed Policies Available for Use with AWS Secrets Manager

This section identifies the AWS managed policies that you can use to help manage access to your secrets. You can't modify or delete an AWS managed policy, but you can attach or detach them to entities in your account as needed.

| Policy Name | Description | ARN |
|---|---|---|
| SecretsManagerReadWrite | Provides access to most Secrets Manager operations. By itself, it doesn't enable configuring rotation because that also requires IAM permissions to create roles. For someone who must configure Lambda rotation functions and enable rotation, you should also assign the IAMFullAccess managed policy. | arn:aws:iam::aws:policy/SecretsManagerReadWrite |

# Actions, Resources, and Context Keys You Can Use in an IAM Policy for AWS Secrets Manager

## Actions That You Can Reference in an IAM Policy

The following table shows the permissions that you can specify in an IAM permissions policy to control access to your secrets. Each permission on an "Action" can be associated with a "Resource" that specifies what the action can work on.

You can restrict use of some actions to only those secrets with Amazon Resource Names (ARNs) that match the `Resource` element in the policy. See the section Resources That You Can Reference in an IAM Policy later in this topic.

If you see an expand arrow () in the upper-right corner of the table, you can open the table in a new window. To close the window, choose the close button (**X**) in the lower-right corner.

| Permission for "Action" element | API operation that's enabled by this action | Resource ARNs that can be used as a "Resource" with this action | Context keys that can be used with this action |
|---|---|---|---|
| secretsmanager:CancelRotateSecret | CancelRotateSecret | Secret | SecretId |
| secretsmanager:CreateSecret | CreateSecret | | Name Description KmsKeyId |
| secretsmanager:DeleteSecret | DeleteSecret | Secret | SecretId VersionId |
| secretsmanager:DescribeSecret | DesecribeSecret | Secret | SecretId |
| secretsmanager:GetRandomPassword | GetRandomPassword | | |
| secretsmanager:GetSecretValue | GetSecretValue | Secret | SecretId VersionId VersionStage |
| secretsmanager:ListSecrets | ListSecrets | | |
| secretsmanager:ListSecretVersionIds | ListSecretVersionIds | Secret | SecretId |
| secretsmanager:PutSecretValue | PutSecretValue | Secret | SecretId |
| secretsmanager:RestoreSecret | RestoreSecret | Secret | SecretId |
| secretsmanager:RotateSecret | RotateSecret | Secret | SecretId RotationLambdaArn |
| secretsmanager:TagResource | TagResource | Secret | SecretId |
| secretsmanager:UntagResource | UntagResource | Secret | SecretId |
| secretsmanager:UpdateSecret | UpdateSecret | Secret | SecretId Description KmsKeyId |
| secretsmanager:UpdateSecretVersionStage | UpdateSecretVersionStage | Secret | SecretId VersionStage |

## Resources That You Can Reference in an IAM Policy

The following table shows the ARN formats that are supported in IAM policies for AWS Secrets Manager. You can view the IDs for each entity on the **Secret details** page for each secret in the Secrets Manager console.

If you see an expand arrow () in the upper-right corner of the table, you can open the table in a new window. To close the window, choose the close button (**X**) in the lower-right corner.

| Resource Type | ARN Format |
|---|---|
| Secret | arn:aws:secretsmanager::*OptionalPath/*SecretName-6RandomCharacters |

Secrets Manager constructs the last part of the ARN by appending a dash and six random alphanumeric characters at the end of your secret's name. This helps ensure that if you ever delete a secret and then recreate another with the same name that individuals with permissions to the original secret don't automatically get access to the new secret because the six random characters will be different.

## Context Keys That You Can Reference in an IAM Policy

Context keys in AWS Secrets Manager generally correspond to the request parameters of an API call. This enables you to allow or block almost any request based on the value of a parameter.

Each context key can be compared using a condition operator to a value that you specify. The context keys that can be used depend on the action selected. See the "Context keys" column in the Actions section at the beginning of this topic.

For example, you could choose to allow someone to retrieve *only* the `AWSCURRENT` version a secret value by using a `Condition` element similar to the following:

```
1    "Effect": "Allow",
2    "Condition": {"StringEqualsIgnoreCase" : {"VersionStage" : "AWSCURRENT"}}
```

The following table shows the context keys that you can specify in the `Condition` element of an IAM permissions policy to more granularly control access to an action.

| Context keys for "Condition" element | Description |
|---|---|
| SecretId | Filters the request based on the unique identifier for the secret that's provided in the SecretId parameter. The value can be either the friendly name or the ARN of the secret. This enables you to limit which secrets can be accessed by a request. |
| Description | Filters the request based on the Description parameter in the request. |
| KmsKeyId | Filters the request based on the KmsKeyId parameter of the request. This enables you to limit which keys can be used in a request. |
| Name | Filters the request based on Name parameter value of the request. This enables you to restrict a secret's name to only those matching this value. |

| Context keys for "Condition" element | Description |
| --- | --- |
| RotationLambdaArn | Filters the request based on the Rotation-LambdaARN parameter. This enables you to restrict which Lambda rotation functions can be used with a secret. It can be used with both CreateSecret and the operations that modify existing secrets. |
| VersionId | Filters the request based on the VersionId parameter of the request. This enables you to restrict which versions of a secret can be accessed. |
| VersionStage | Filters the request based on the staging labels that are identified in the VersionStage parameter of a request. This enables you to restrict access to only the secret versions that have a staging label that matches one of the values in this string array parameter. Because this is a multi-valued string array, you must use one of the set operators to compare strings with this value. |
| resource/AllowRotationLambda | Filters the request based on the ARN of the Lambda rotation function attached to the resource that the request is targeting. This enables you to restrict access to only those secrets that already have a rotation Lambda ARN that matches this value. |
| resourcetag/tagname | Filters the request based on a tag attached to the secret. Replace tagname with the actual tag name. You can then use condition operators to ensure that the tag is present, and that it has the requested value. |

# Troubleshooting AWS Secrets Manager

If you encounter issues when working with AWS Secrets Manager, consult the topics in this section.

**Topics**

- Troubleshooting General Issues
- Troubleshooting AWS Secrets Manager Rotation of Secrets

# Troubleshooting General Issues

Use the information here to help you diagnose and fix access-denied or other common issues that you might encounter when you're working with AWS Secrets Manager.

**Topics**

- I get an "access denied" message when I make a request to AWS Secrets Manager.
- I get an "access denied" message when I make a request with temporary security credentials.
- Changes that I make aren't always immediately visible.

## I get an "access denied" message when I make a request to AWS Secrets Manager.

- Verify that you have permissions to call the operation and resource that you've requested. An administrator must grant permissions by attaching an IAM policy to your IAM user, or to a group that you're a member of. If the policy statements that grant those permissions include any conditions, such as time-of-day or IP address restrictions, you also must meet those requirements when you send the request. For information about viewing or modifying policies for an IAM user, group, or role, see Working with Policies in the *IAM User Guide*.
- If you're signing API requests manually (without using the AWS SDKs), verify that you've correctly signed the request.

## I get an "access denied" message when I make a request with temporary security credentials.

- Verify that the IAM user or role that you're using to make the request has the correct permissions. Permissions for temporary security credentials are derived from an IAM user or role. This means that the permissions are limited to those that are granted to the IAM user or role. For more information about how permissions for temporary security credentials are determined, see Controlling Permissions for Temporary Security Credentials in the *IAM User Guide*.
- Verify that your requests are being signed correctly and that the request is well-formed. For details, see the toolkit documentation for your chosen SDK, or Using Temporary Security Credentials to Request Access to AWS Resources in the *IAM User Guide*.
- Verify that your temporary security credentials haven't expired. For more information, see Requesting Temporary Security Credentials in the *IAM User Guide*.

## Changes that I make aren't always immediately visible.

As a service that's accessed through computers in data centers around the world, AWS Secrets Manager uses a distributed computing model called eventual consistency. Any change that you make in Secrets Manager (or other AWS services) takes time to become visible from all possible endpoints. Some of the delay results from the time it takes to send the data from server to server, from replication zone to replication zone, and from region to region around the world. Secrets Manager also uses caching to improve performance, but in some cases this can add time. The change might not be visible until the previously cached data times out.

Design your global applications to account for these potential delays. Also, ensure that they work as expected, even when a change made in one location isn't instantly visible at another.

For more information about how some other AWS services are affected by this, consult the following resources:

- Managing Data Consistency in the *Amazon Redshift Database Developer Guide*
- Amazon S3 Data Consistency Model in the *Amazon Simple Storage Service Developer Guide*
- Ensuring Consistency When Using Amazon S3 and Amazon Elastic MapReduce for ETL Workflows in the AWS Big Data Blog

- EC2 Eventual Consistency in the *Amazon EC2 API Reference*

# Troubleshooting AWS Secrets Manager Rotation of Secrets

Use the information here to help you diagnose and fix common errors that you might encounter when you're rotating Secrets Manager secrets.

Rotating secrets in AWS Secrets Manager requires you to use a Lambda function that defines how to interact with the database or service that owns the secret.

**Topics**

- I want to find the diagnostic logs for my Lambda rotation function
- I get "access denied" when trying to configure rotation for my secret
- My first rotation fails after I enable rotation
- Secrets Manager says I successfully configured rotation, but the password isn't rotating
- CloudTrail shows access-denied errors during rotation

## I want to find the diagnostic logs for my Lambda rotation function

When the rotation function isn't operating the way that you expect, the first thing you should check are the logs. Secrets Manager provides template code for the Lambda rotation function, and this code writes error messages to the CloudWatch log.

**To view the CloudWatch logs for your Lambda function**

1. Open the AWS Lambda console at https://console.aws.amazon.com/lambda/.

2. From the list of functions, choose the name of the Lambda function that's associated with your secret.

3. Choose the **Monitoring** tab.

4. In the **Invocation errors** section, choose **Jump to Logs**.

   The CloudWatch console opens and displays the logs for your function.

## I get "access denied" when trying to configure rotation for my secret

When you add a Lambda rotation function's Amazon Resource Name (ARN) to your secret, Secrets Manager checks the permissions of the function. The role policy for the function must grant the Secrets Manager service principal `secretsmanager.amazonaws.com` permission to invoke the function (`lambda:InvokeFunction`).

You can add this permission by running the following AWS CLI command:

```
1 aws lambda add-permission --function-name ARN_of_lambda_function --principal secretsmanager.
    amazonaws.com --action lambda:InvokeFunction --statement-id SecretsManagerAccess
```

## My first rotation fails after I enable rotation

When you enable rotation for a secret that uses a "master" secret to change the credentials on the secured service, Secrets Manager automatically configures most elements that are required for rotation. However, Secrets Manager can't automatically grant permission to read the master secret to your Lambda function. You must explicitly grant this permission yourself. Specifically, you grant the permission by adding it to the policy attached to the IAM role that's attached to your Lambda rotation function. That policy must include the following statement (this is only a statement, not a complete policy). For the complete policy, see the second sample policy in the section CloudTrail shows access-denied errors during rotation.

```
1 {
2     "Sid": "AllowAccessToMasterSecret",
3     "Effect": "Allow",
4     "Action": "secretsmanager:GetSecretValue",
5     "Resource": "ARN_of_master_secret"
6 }
```

This enables the rotation function to retrieve the credentials from the master secret—which it can then use to change the credentials for the secret being rotated.

## Secrets Manager says I successfully configured rotation, but the password isn't rotating

This can occur if there are network configuration issues that prevent the Lambda function from communicating with either your secured database/service or the Secrets Manager service endpoint (which is on the public internet). If your database/service is running in a VPC, then you can configure things one of two ways:

- Make the database in the VPC publicly accessible with an Amazon EC2 Elastic IP address.
- Configure the Lambda rotation function to operate in the same VPC as the database/service. In this case, your VPC must be equipped with a NAT gateway so that the Lambda rotation function can reach the public Secrets Manager service endpoint.

To determine if this type of configuration issue is the cause of the rotation failure, perform the following steps:

**To diagnose connectivity issues between your rotation function and the database or Secrets Manager**

1. Open your logs by following the procedure I want to find the diagnostic logs for my Lambda rotation function.

2. Examine the log files to look for indications that there are timeouts occurring between either the Lambda function and the AWS Secrets Manager service, or between the Lambda function and the secured database or service.

3. For information about how to configure services and Lambda functions to interoperate within the VPC environment, see the Amazon Virtual Private Cloud documentation and the AWS Lambda Developer Guide .

## CloudTrail shows access-denied errors during rotation

When you configure rotation, if you let Secrets Manager create the rotation function for you, it's automatically provided with a policy attached to the function's IAM role that grants the appropriate permissions. If you create the function on your own, you need to grant the following permissions to the role that's attached to the function.

```
1 {
2     "Version": "2012-10-17",
3     "Statement": [
4         {
5             "Effect": "Allow",
6             "Action": [
7                 "secretsmanager:DescribeSecret",
8                 "secretsmanager:GetRandomPassword",
9                 "secretsmanager:GetSecretValue",
10                "secretsmanager:PutSecretValue",
11                "secretsmanager:UpdateSecretVersionStage"
12            ],
```

```
13            "Resource": "*"
14        }
15    ]
16 }
```

Also, if your rotation uses separate master secret credentials to rotate this secret, then you must also grant permission to retrieve the secret value from the master secret. For more information, see My first rotation fails after I enable rotation. The combined policy might look like this:

```
1  {
2      "Version": "2012-10-17",
3      "Statement": [
4          {
5              "Sid": "AllowAccessToSecretsManagerAPIs",
6              "Effect": "Allow",
7              "Action": [
8                  "secretsmanager:DescribeSecret",
9                  "secretsmanager:GetRandomPassword",
10                 "secretsmanager:GetSecretValue",
11                 "secretsmanager:PutSecretValue",
12                 "secretsmanager:UpdateSecretVersionStage",
13             ],
14             "Resource": "*"
15         },
16         {
17             "Sid": "AllowAccessToMasterSecret",
18             "Effect": "Allow",
19             "Action": "secretsmanager:GetSecretValue",
20             "Resource": "ARN_of_master_secret"
21         }
22     ]
23 }
```

# Calling the API by Making HTTP Query Requests

This section contains general information about using the Query API for AWS Secrets Manager. For details about the API operations and errors, see the AWS Secrets Manager API Reference.

**Note**
Instead of making direct calls to the AWS Secrets Manager Query API, you can use one of the AWS SDKs. The AWS SDKs consist of libraries and sample code for various programming languages and platforms (Java, Ruby, .NET, iOS, Android, and more). The SDKs provide a convenient way to create programmatic access to Secrets Manager and AWS. For example, the SDKs take care of tasks such as cryptographically signing requests, managing errors, and retrying requests automatically. For information about the AWS SDKs, including how to download and install them, see Tools for Amazon Web Services.

The Query API for AWS Secrets Manager lets you call service operations. Query API requests are HTTPS requests that must contain an `Action` parameter to indicate the operation to be performed. AWS Secrets Manager supports GET and POST requests for all operations. That is, the API doesn't require you to use GET for some operations and POST for others. However, GET requests are subject to the limitation size of a URL. Although this limit is browser dependent, a typical limit is 2048 bytes. Therefore, for Query API requests that require larger sizes, you must use a POST request.

The response is an XML document. For details about the response, see the individual API description pages in the AWS Organizations API Reference.

**Topics**
- Endpoints
- HTTPS Required
- Signing API Requests for Secrets Manager

## Endpoints

AWS Secrets Manager has endpoints in most AWS Regions. For the complete list, see the endpoint list for AWS Secrets Manager in the *AWS General Reference*.

For more information about AWS Regions and endpoints for all services, see Regions and Endpoints, also in the *AWS General Reference*.

## HTTPS Required

Because the Query API returns sensitive information such as security credentials, you must use HTTPS to encrypt all API requests.

## Signing API Requests for Secrets Manager

You must sign API requests by using an access key ID and a secret access key. We strongly recommend that you don't use your AWS account's root user credentials for everyday work with Secrets Manager. Instead, you can use the credentials for an IAM user, or temporary credentials like you use with an IAM role.

To sign your API requests, you must use AWS Signature Version 4. For information about using Signature Version 4, see Signature Version 4 Signing Process in the *AWS General Reference*.

For more information, see the following:

- AWS Security Credentials. Provides general information about the types of credentials that you can use to access AWS.

- IAM Best Practices. Offers suggestions for using the IAM service to help secure your AWS resources, including those in Secrets Manager.
- Temporary Credentials. Describes how to create and use temporary security credentials.

# Document History for AWS Secrets Manager

The following table describes major documentation updates for AWS Secrets Manager.

- **API version: 2017-10-17**

| Change | Description | Date |
|---|---|---|
| Compliance with HIPAA | Secrets Manager is now available as a HIPAA eligible service. | June 4, 2018 |
| Initial release of service | Documentation is provided for the initial release of AWS Secrets Manager. | April 4, 2018 |

# AWS Glossary

For the latest AWS terminology, see the AWS Glossary in the *AWS General Reference*.